# TECHNOLOGY VS. HUMANITY

## The coming clash between man and machine

## Gerd Leonhard

www.fastfuturepublishing.com

*This book is dedicated to my dear wife, Angelica Feldmann, who taught me so much about humanity, lovingly endured my absence during the writing of it, provided much-needed and honest critique, and supported me all the way. Without you, this book would not exist.*

TECHNOLOGY vs. HUMANITY

First published in United Kingdom and
United States of America by
Fast Future Publishing Ltd 2016

FutureScapes is an imprint of
Fast Future Publishing Ltd 2016
www.fastfuturepublishing.com

For information contact info@fastfuturepublishing.com

Paperback ISBN 978 0 9932958 2 9
Ebook 978 0 9932958 3 6

FutureScapes Series Editors - Rohit Talwar, Steve Wells and April Koury

Art Director - Jean Francois Cardella

Book cover: www.angellondon.co.uk

Print production by Print Trail
printtrail.com

# Table of Contents

# Introduction

*How can humanness prevail in the face of exponential and all-encompassing technological change?*

Our world is entering a period of truly transformative change where many of us will be surprised by the scale and pace of developments we simply hadn't anticipated. These exponential technological advances offer tremendous potential, and with these opportunities come tremendous new responsibilities.

## Humanity's biggest challenge

I believe the scale of change caused by recent, unforeseen events such as Brexit (the UK's June 2016 referendum decision to leave the European Union) will be miniscule compared to the impact of an avalanche of technological change that could reshape the very essence of humanity and every aspect of life on our planet.

In the past, each radical shift in human society has been driven primarily by one key enabling shift factor—from wood, stone, bronze, and iron, to steam, electricity, factory automation, and the Internet. Today, however, I see a set of science and technology enabled Megashifts coming together that will redraw not only commerce, culture, and society, but also our biology and our ethics.

## A manifesto for furthering human flourishing

Let me be clear: Technology vs. Humanity is neither a celebration of the rapidly onrushing technology revolution nor a lament on the fall of civilization. If, like me, you're a film buff, then you've probably already had more than enough of Hollywood's utopian visions and dystopian warnings. The future cannot be created based on blind optimism or paralyzing fear!

My goal with this book is to amplify and accelerate the debate about how to ensure that we guide, harness, and control science and technology developments so that they fulfill their primary purpose, which should be serving humanity and furthering human flourishing.

My ambition is to take the discussion beyond the realms of the exuberant technologists, serious academics, and thoughtful analysts to express a set of concerns that are nowhere near to being addressed or even recognized by the population at large. As a futurist—and increasingly more of a nowist—I am also hoping to give real presence and current urgency to a future that seems beyond comprehension and unworthy of attention for many.

As such, this book is deliberately designed to be a passionate discussion starter for what I consider to be the world's most important conversation. I believe my role here is to open up and catalyze the debate; hence, I have set out to craft a spirited manifesto rather than a blueprint or "how to" guidebook. To help stimulate and further that debate, I will expand on the themes outlined in the book through my future talks, online contributions, and films.

### Just because we can, it doesn't mean we should

I believe we need to step back from an expert-led debate about what's possible and how to achieve it. Instead, I think we must start with a more fundamental exploration of what role we want these transformative technologies to play in serving humanity: Just because we can, it doesn't mean we should.

To help guide this exploration, I have set out what I believe to be the driving forces of change, and presented an assessment of their potential impacts and implications. I have highlighted many fundamental questions raised by the accelerated—and in many cases exponential—pace of development across multiple fields of science and technology.

I argue that we must place human happiness and well-being at the heart of the decision making and governance processes that will shape future investments in scientific and technological research, development, and commercialization because, in the end, technology is not what we seek, but how we seek.

I go on to present a range of different scenarios on how things might play out depending on the development path we take to the future. I conclude with a starter set of straw man ideas to kick-start discussions on how to choose the best path for humanity, and how to make good decisions along the way.

To open up this ambitious conversation and help guide the discussion, I have structured my thoughts into twelve key chapters:

*Chapter 1: A Prologue to the Future* – Halfway through the century's second decade we are at a critical pivot point in technology evolution, a hinge moment when change will not only become combinatory and exponential but inevitable and irreversible. Here I argue that now is our last chance to question the nature of these coming challenges, from artificial intelligence to human genome editing. Striking a balance will be the key.

*Chapter 2: Tech vs. Us* – In this chapter, I explain why technology may increasingly simulate and replace—but can never become or be us. Technology has no ethics, and therefore its imminent entry into our most private lives and biological processes must be negotiated as a top civic and corporate priority. I examine the nature of ethics as a human signifier and differentiator, transcending differences of religion and culture.

*Chapter 3: The Megashifts* – Digital transformation is being touted as the paradigm shift *du jour* across enterprises and the public sector—when in fact it is just one of ten Megashifts that will interact and alter the face of human life forever. I explore these Megashifts— from mobilization and automation to robotization. These are not slow evolutionary processes which we will have time to integrate and adapt to. Rather, they will trigger a tsunami of disruption and change, potentially equating to a mass extinction event for much of the existing global commerce infrastructure.

*Chapter 4: Automating Society* – This chapter challenges the pervasive and seriously misleading myth that automation will only disrupt blue-collar—or even white-collar—labor. The coming wave of automation will move way beyond the factory or public infrastructure and into our very biological processes such as aging and even giving birth. Used as we are to the gradual societal shifts brought about by previous change waves, often allowing decades to adjust and respond, I ask if we as a tribe are ready to abdicate our human sovereignty to the faceless forces of technology? Are you ready for the biggest loss of free will and individual human control in history?

*Chapter 5: The Internet of Inhuman Things* – This chapter explores the potential challenges posed by the Internet of Things—the current dominant narrative within digital transformation, with thousands of corporate strategies riding on its tailwinds. Have we paused to ask ourselves the difference between algorithms and what makes us essentially human—what I call the androrithms? Will the Internet of Inhuman Things gradually and then suddenly require us to forgo our humanity and become ever more mechanistic just to remain relevant? As computing becomes mobile, then wearable, and soon ingestible or implantable, will our distinct planetary advantage as a species be sacrificed for a spurious digital hit?

*Chapter 6: Magic to Manic to Toxic* – Here I examine how our love affair with tech often follows a predictable curve from magic to manic to—ultimately—toxic. As we allow ourselves to experience life as an ever more mediated and processed sequence of encounters, we may think we are enjoying ourselves, but in reality we are simply being hot-wired by our hormones—hormones increasingly targeted by the gentle purveyors of "big tech." As we rave through the all-night honeymoon party that is technological progress, it's salutary to think about the hangover—the price to be paid tomorrow, and forever.

*Chapter 7: Digital Obesity: Our Latest Pandemic* – This chapter discusses how digital obesity may not be as currently familiar as the physical kind, but is rapidly developing into a pandemic of unprecedented proportions. As we wallow and pig out on a glut of news, updates, and algorithmically engineered information, we also entertain ourselves in a burgeoning tech-bubble of questionable entertainment. Taking into account the coming tidal wave of new technologies and digital engagement platforms, it's high time to think about digital nutrition just as we already do about bodily nurture.

*Chapter 8: Precaution vs. Proaction* – This chapter sets out the argument that the safest—and still most promising—future is one where we do not postpone innovation, but neither do we dismiss the exponential risks it now involves and hand it off as "somebody else's problem." The bill passed on to the next generation for today's new technology gambles cannot be postponed—any downside will be immediate and unprecedented in scale. I argue that precaution and proaction, the two principles often deployed to date, are both insufficient to deal with a combinatory, exponential scenario where waiting will be as dangerous as firing ahead. Transhumanism—with its lemming-like rush to the edge of the unknown—represents the scariest of all present options.

*Chapter 9: Taking the Happenstance out of Happiness* – Money talks, but happiness remains the bigger story. Happiness is not only considered the ultimate goal of human existence across philosophies and cultures, it also remains an elusive factor resistant to exact measurement or technological replication. As big tech simulates the quick hits of hedonistic pleasure, how can we protect the deeper forms of happiness that involve empathy, compassion, and consciousness? Happiness is also related to luck, to happenstance—but how will we use technology to limit the risks of human life and still preserve its mystery and spontaneity?

*Chapter 10: Digital Ethics* – In this chapter, I argue that, as technology permeates every aspect of human life and activity, digital ethics will evolve into a burning, un-ignorable issue for every individual and organization. At present we do not even have a common global language to discuss the issue, let alone agreement on accepted rights and responsibilities. Environmental sustainability is often brushed aside by the developing economies as a first world problem and is always sidetracked during economic recessions. In contrast, digital ethics will force its way to a permanent position at the front and center of our political and economic lives. It's time to have the ethical conversation about digital technology—a potentially greater threat to continued human flourishing than nuclear proliferation.

*Chapter 11: Earth 2030: Heaven or Hell?* – As we move imaginatively into the near and medium future, we can easily visualize some of the gigantic changes altering work and life out of all recognition—these are explored here. Many of these seismic changes are to be welcomed per se—like working for a passion rather than for a living. However, many of the most basic privileges we once took for granted, like freedom of choice in consumption and independent free will in lifestyle, could become vestigial echoes or the preserves of ultra high-net-worth individuals. Heaven or hell? Make your choice, but do it now.

*Chapter 12: Decision Time* – In this closing chapter I argue that it's crunch time for tech adoption—not the application of technology itself, but the deeper integration and delineation of technology in human life. Numerous ethical, economic, social, and biological issues will simply not wait for another forum or the next generation. It's time to regulate mass technology application just as we would any other transformational force such as nuclear power. This is not the conclusion of a rich dialogue, but the beginning of a conversation that needs to become mainstream in our media, our schools, our government, and—most immediately—our boardrooms. The time for technologists and technocrats to simply hand the ethical buck over to someone else has passed.

I hope that this book inspires you to think deeply about the challenges we face, and I invite you to contribute to this conversation by becoming a member of the techvshuman/TVH community at www.techvshuman.com.

*Gerd Leonhard*
*Zurich, Switzerland*
*August 2016*

# Chapter 1
# A Prologue to the Future

*Humanity will change more in the next*
*20 years than in the previous 300 years.*

Human beings have a habit of extrapolating the future from the present, or even the past. The assumption is that whatever worked well for us up to now should, in some slightly improved shape or form, also serve us nicely in the future. Yet the new reality is that, because of the increased impact of exponential and combinatorial technological changes, the future is actually very unlikely to be an extension of the present. Rather, it is certain to be utterly different—because the assumption framework and the underlying logic have changed.

Therefore, in my work as a futurist I try to intuit, imagine, and immerse myself in the near future (five to eight years out), present views from that world, and then work my way back to the present from there rather than towards it.

Starting with a report from that near future, this book goes on to explore the challenges and lay out a manifesto, a passionate call to stop and think before we all get swept up in the magic vortex of technology, and eventually become fundamentally less rather than more human. This is a good time to remember that the future does not just happen to us—it is created by us, every day, and we will be held responsible for the decisions we make at this very moment.

## A historic inflection point

I feel that we are living in one of the most exciting times in the history of mankind, and I am generally very optimistic about the future. However, we definitely need to define and practice a more holistic approach to technology governance in order to safeguard the very essence of what being human means.

We are at the inflection point of an exponential curve in many fields of science and technology (S&T), a point where the doubling from each measurement period to the next is becoming vastly more significant.

At the heart of the story of exponential change lies Moore's Law—a concept which originated in the 1970s, and which, simply put, suggests that the processing speed (i.e. the amount of computer processing power on a chip) that we can buy for US$1,000 doubles roughly every 18–24 months.[1]

This exponential pace of development is now evident in fields as diverse as deep learning, genetics, material sciences, and manufacturing. The time required for each exponential performance step is also declining in many fields, and this is driving the potential for fundamental change across every activity on the planet. In practical terms, we are now past the stage in the life of the curve where it was difficult to gauge that something is happening at all, i.e. we are no longer moving in small steps from 0.01 to 0.02 or 0.04 to 0.08.

At the same time, fortunately, we are not yet at the point where those doublings are so great that the results will overwhelm our understanding and inhibit our capacity to act. To put things in perspective, in my view we are at a relative performance level of around four in most fields, and the next exponential step will take us to eight, rather than a more linear rise to five! This is the very moment when exponential increases are starting to really matter, and technology is now driving exponential changes in every sector of our society, from energy, transportation, communications, and media, to medicine, health, food, and energy.

Witness the recent changes in the car industry—during the past seven years we've gone from electric cars with a range of less than 50 miles to the latest Tesla and BMWi8 promising over 300 miles on a single charge.[2][3] We've also gone from a handful of charging locations to the astounding fact that New York City already has more electric vehicle (EV) charging stations than gas stations.[4] Nearly every month there's a new breakthrough in battery efficiency, a limitation which has for the past decades been one of the biggest barriers to mass adoption of EVs. Soon we'll charge our EVs just once a week, then once a month, and eventually maybe just once a year—and then it seems likely that very few people will still be interested in huge luxury cars with good old gas engines!

Witness the even more dramatic cost decline in human genome sequencing, with the price falling from around US$10 million in 2008 to approximately US$800 today.[5] Imagine what might happen when exponentially more powerful supercomputers move into the cloud and become available to every medical facility or lab: The cost of sequencing an individual's genome should quickly drop below US$50.[6]

Next, imagine the genome profiles of some two billion people uploaded to a secure cloud (hopefully in an anonymized way!) for use in research, development, and analysis—much of it performed by artificial intelligence (AI) running on those very same supercomputers. The scientific possibilities that will be unleashed will blow away anything we have dreamed of, while simultaneously bringing enormous ethical challenges: dramatic longevity increases for those that have the budget, the ability to reprogram the human genome, and—potentially—the end of aging, or even dying. Will the rich live forever while the poor still can't even afford malaria pills?

Such exponential developments suggest that continuing to imagine our future in a linear way will probably lead to catastrophically flawed assumptions about the scale, speed, and potential impacts of change. That may be part of the reason why so many people cannot seem to grasp the growing concerns about technology trumping humanity— it all seems so far away, and, for now, rather harmless because we are only at four on this curve. Issues such as the increasing loss of privacy, technological unemployment, or human deskilling are still not in-our-faces enough—but this is bound to change very quickly.

It is also important to realize that the biggest shifts will happen because of combinatorial innovation, i.e. by the simultaneous exploitation of several Megashifts and elements of disruption. For example, in chapter 3, we'll discuss how we are increasingly seeing companies combining big data and the Internet of Things (IoT) along with AI, mobility, and the cloud to create extremely disruptive new offerings.

Suffice to say that nothing and no one will be untouched by the changes in store for us, whether they are realized with good will, while ignoring or neglecting to consider the unintended consequences, or with harmful intent. On the one hand, unimaginable technological breakthroughs may dramatically improve our lives and hugely further human flourishing (see chapter 9); on the other, some of these exponential technological changes are likely to threaten the very fabric of society and ultimately challenge our very humanness.

In 1993, computer scientist and famed science fiction author Vernor Vinge wrote:

> Within 30 years, we will have the technological means to create superhuman intelligence. Shortly after, the human era will be ended. Is such progress avoidable? If not to be avoided, can events be guided so that we may survive?[7]

## Welcome to HellVen!

It is becoming clearer that the future of human-machine relations very much depends on the economic system that creates them. We are facing what I like to call HellVen (i.e. a blend of hell/heaven) challenges (#hellven). We are moving at warp speed towards a world that may resemble Nirvana, where we may no longer have to work for a living, most problems are solved by technology, and we enjoy a kind of universal abundance—sometimes referred to as the *Star Trek* economy.[8]

However, the future could also usher in a dystopian society that is orchestrated and overseen by supercomputers, networked bots, and super-intelligent software agents—machines and algorithms, cyborgs and robots—or rather, by those who own them. A world where non-augmented humans might be tolerated as pets or as a necessary nuisance at best, or, at worst, enslaved by a cabal of cyborg gods; a dark society that would be deskilled, desensitized, disembodied, and altogether dehumanized.

> *"You may live to see man-made horrors beyond your comprehension." –Nikola Tesla*[9]

### Is this a paranoid view?

Let's consider what some of us are already witnessing in our daily lives: Low-cost, ubiquitous digital technologies have made it possible for us to outsource our thinking, our decisions, and our memories to ever-cheaper mobile devices and the intelligent clouds behind them. These "external brains" are morphing quickly from knowing-me to representing-me to being-me. In fact, they are starting to become a digital copy of us—and if that thought is not worrying you yet, imagine the power of this external brain amplified 100x in the next five years.

Navigating a strange city? Impossible without Google Maps. Can't decide where to eat tonight? TripAdvisor will tell me. No time to answer all my emails? Gmail's new intelligent assistant will do it for me.[10]

As far as man-machine convergence is concerned, we're not quite in a land where we stay at home while our cyborg doubles live out our lives for us, as in the 2009 Bruce Willis film *Surrogates*.[11] Nor are we yet able to purchase human-like synths that can undertake a range of tasks and provide companionship as in the 2015 AMC TV series *Humans*[12]—but we're not that far away either.

In this book I will explain why I do not think the dystopian scenario is likely to happen. At the same time, I will argue that we are now facing some fundamental choices when it comes to deciding and planning how far we will allow technology to impact and shape our lives, the lives of our loved ones, and the lives of future generations. Some pundits may say we are already beyond the point of preventing such changes, and that this is just the next stage in our "natural" evolution. I strongly disagree and will explain how I think humans can emerge as winners in this coming clash between man and machines.

## Technology and humanity are converging, and we are at a pivot point

As I started writing this book and weaving the themes into my talks, three important words rose to the top and stood out—exponential, combinatorial, and recursive.

1. **Exponential.** Technology is progressing exponentially. Even though the basic laws of physics may prevent microchips from becoming significantly smaller than they already are today, technological progress in general is still following Moore's Law.[13] The performance curve continues to rise exponentially, rather than in the gradual or linear way humans tend to understand and expect. This represents a huge cognitive challenge for us: Technology grows exponentially, while humans (hopefully, I would add) remain linear.

2. **Combinatorial.** Technological advances are being combined and integrated. Game-changing advances such as machine intelligence and deep learning, the IoT, and human genome editing are beginning to intersect and amplify each other. They are no longer applied just in specific individual domains—instead they are causing ripples across a multitude of sectors. For example, advanced human gene editing technologies such as CRISPR-Cas9 may eventually allow us to beat cancer and dramatically increase longevity.[14] These are developments that would upend the entire logic of healthcare, social security, work, and even capitalism itself.

**3. Recursive.** Technologies such as AI, cognitive computing, and deep learning may eventually lead to recursive (i.e. self-amplifying) improvements. For example, we are already seeing the first examples of robots that can reprogram or upgrade themselves or control the power grid that keeps them alive, potentially leading to what has been called an intelligence explosion. Some, such as Oxford academic Nick Bostrom, believe this could lead to the emergence of super-intelligence—AI systems which could one day learn faster and out-think humans in almost every regard.[15] If we can engineer AIs with an IQ of 500, what would keep us from building others with an IQ of 50,000—and what could happen if we did?

Thankfully, recursive super-intelligence is not yet on the immediate horizon. However, even without such challenges, we are already grappling with some rapidly escalating issues, such as the constant tracking of our digital lives, surveillance-by-default, diminishing privacy, the loss of anonymity, digital identity theft, data security, and much more. That is why I am convinced the groundwork for the future of humanity—positive or dystopian—is being laid here, today.

We are at a crucial junction, and we must act with much greater foresight, with a decidedly more holistic view, and with much stronger stewardship as we unleash technologies that could end up having infinitely more power over us than we could ever imagine.

We can no longer adopt a wait-and-see attitude if we want to remain in control of our destiny and the developments that could shape it. Rather, we must pay equally as much attention to what it will mean to be or remain human in the future (i.e. what defines us as humans) as we spend on developing infinitely more powerful technologies that will change humanity forever.

We should take great care to not just leave these decisions to "free markets," to venture capitalists, corporate technologists, or the world's most powerful military organizations. The future of humanity should not be about some generic, Industrial Age paradigm of profit and growth at all costs, or some outmoded technological imperative that may have served us well in the 1980s. Neither Silicon Valley nor the world's most technologized nations should end up becoming "mission control for humanity" just because technology generates vast new revenue streams and large profits.

Thankfully, I believe we are still at a 90/10 point right now: 90% of the amazing possibilities presented by technology could play out well for humanity, while 10% might already be troublesome or negative. If we can maintain that balance, or bring it up to 98/2, that would be worth every effort. At the same time, that troubling 10% (even if mostly unintended at this time) may quickly balloon to 50% or more if we do not agree on exactly how we want these technologies to serve humanity. This is clearly not a good time to just "push ahead and see what happens."

## Artificial intelligence and human genome editing are the two primary game changers

The first major force in the realm of exponential technologies is AI, simply defined as creating machines (software or robots) that are intelligent and capable of self-learning—i.e. more human-like thinking machines. The capability of AI is widely projected to grow twice as fast as all other technologies, exceeding Moore's Law and the growth of computing power, in general.[16]

*"By far the greatest danger of artificial intelligence is that people conclude too early that they understand it." –Eliezer Yudkowsky[17]*

The companion game changer to AI is human genome engineering: altering human DNA to put an end to some if not all diseases, reprogram our bodies, and possibly even end death. Indeed, AI will be a critical enabler of such reprogramming.

These two game changers and their scientific neighbors will have huge impact on what humans can and will be in less than 20 years. In this book, in the interests of brevity, I will focus in particular on AI and deep learning because of their immediate relevance to our future and their enabling role in the development of other "game changer" fields such as human genome editing, nanotechnology and material sciences.

## Becoming as God?

Dr. Ray Kurzweil, currently Google's Director of Engineering, is a great influence on futurist thinking in general and on my own work, but also someone whose views I must often challenge in this book. Kurzweil predicts that computers will surpass the processing power of a single human brain by 2025, and that a single computer may match the power of all human brains combined by 2050.[18]

Kurzweil suggests these developments will herald the advent of the so-called Singularity, the moment when computers finally trump and then surpass human brains in computing power. This is the moment when human intelligence may become increasingly nonbiological, when it may be possible for machines to independently, and quite likely recursively, go beyond their original programming—a decisive moment in human history.

Ray Kurzweil told his audience at Singularity University in late 2015:

> As we evolve, we become closer to God. Evolution is a spiritual process. There is beauty and love and creativity and intelligence in the world—it all comes from the neocortex. So we're going to expand the brain's neocortex and become more godlike.[19]

I also believe the point of computers having the capacity of the human brain is not far off, but—God or no God—unlike Dr. Kurzweil, I do not think we should willingly give up our humanness in return for the possibility of attaining unlimited nonbiological intelligence. That strikes me as a very bad bargain, a downgrade rather than an upgrade, and in this book I will explain why I passionately believe we should not go down that road.

Right now, in 2016, computers simply do not have the power to deliver on Kurzweil's vision. I believe the chips are still too big, networks still do not have the speed, and the electricity grid by and large cannot support machines that would need this much power. Obviously, these are temporary hurdles: Every day we hear announcements of major scientific breakthroughs and, in addition, numerous unpublicized advances are certain to be happening in secret in labs around the world.

We need to be ready for the Singularity: open yet critical, scientific yet humanistic, adventurous and curious yet armed with precaution, and entrepreneurial yet collectively-minded.

### Science fiction is becoming science fact

Very soon, machines will be able to do things that once were the sole domain of human workers—blue collar and white collar alike—such as understanding language, complex image recognition, or using our body in highly flexible and adaptive ways. By then, we will no doubt be utterly dependent on machines in every aspect of our lives. We will also likely see a rapid merging of man and machine via new types of interfaces such as augmented reality (AR), virtual reality (VR), holograms, implants, brain-computer interfaces (BCI), and body parts engineered with nanotechnology and synthetic biology.

If and when things such as nanobots in our bloodstream or communications implants in our brains become possible, who will decide what is human? If (as I like to say) technology does not (and probably should not) have ethics, what will happen with our norms, social contracts, values, and morals when machines run everything for us?

For the foreseeable future, despite the claims of AI evangelists, I believe machine intelligence will not include emotional intelligence or ethical concerns, because machines are not beings—they are duplicators and simulators. Yet eventually, machines will be able to read, analyze, and possibly understand our value systems, social contracts, ethics, and beliefs—but they will never be able to exist in, or be a part of, the world as we are (what German philosophers like to call *dasein*).

But regardless, will we live in a world where data and algorithms triumph over what I call androrithms, all that stuff that makes us human? (I will define exactly what I believe an androrithm is later in this book.)

Again, successive doublings from 4 to 8 to 16 to 32 are a whole lot different in impact than the doublings from 0.1 to 0.8. This is one of our toughest challenges today: We must imagine an exponentially different tomorrow, and we must become stewards of a future whose complexity may well go far beyond current human understanding. In a way, we must become exponentially imaginative.

### Gradually, then suddenly

For me, this line from Ernest Hemingway's *The Sun Also Rises* describes the nature of exponential change perfectly:[20]

"How did you go bankrupt?"
"Two ways. Gradually, then suddenly."

When thinking about creating our future, it is essential to understand these twin memes of exponentiality and gradually then suddenly, and both are key messages in this book. Increasingly, we will see the humble beginnings of a huge opportunity or threat. And then, all of a sudden, it is either gone and forgotten or it is here, now, and much bigger than imagined. Think of solar energy, autonomous vehicles, digital currencies, and the blockchain: All took a long time to play out, but all of a sudden, they are here and they are roaring. History tells us that those who adapt too slowly or fail to foresee the pivot points will suffer the consequences.

Wait and see is very likely going to mean waiting to become irrelevant, or simply to be ignored, outmoded, and to wither away. Thus, we need another strategy for defining and retaining what makes us human in this quickly digitizing world.

I tend to think that markets will not self-regulate and deal with these issues by means of an "invisible hand." Rather, traditional profit-and-growth-driven open markets will only escalate the challenges of humanity versus technology because these very same technologies are likely to generate opportunities worth trillions of dollars per year. Replacing human qualities, interactions, or idiosyncrasies with technology is simply too much of a business opportunity to question. For example, Peter Diamandis, a board member of a California company aptly called Human Longevity Inc., often proclaims that increasing longevity would create a US$3.5 trillion global market.[21] These irresistible new frontiers are likely to trump any such minor concern as the future of humanness.

### Beyond mission control

In the end, we are talking about the survival and the flourishing of the human species, and I believe it just won't do to have venture capitalists, stock markets, and the military running the show on their own.

In the near future, we are certain to see some very tough battles between opposing world-views and paradigms with gigantic economic interests facing off against each other, a kind of humanists versus transhumanists' showdown. Now that oil and other fossil fuels are declining as the driving force of politics and military concerns, the US and China are already at the forefront of an accelerating technological arms race. The new wars will be digital, and the battle is being waged for leadership in exponential game changers such as AI, human genome modification, the IoT, cyber security, and digital warfare. Europe (including and especially Switzerland, where I live) is somewhat stuck in the middle, more concerned with what many would see as lofty issues such as human rights, happiness, balance, ethics, and sustainable and collective well-being. As I'll explain, I believe addressing these concerns is actually our big opportunity here in Europe.

There are already global tribes of opinion leaders, serial entrepreneurs, scientists, venture capitalists, and assorted tech gurus (and yes, futurists as well) busy promoting a quick voluntary departure from humanism altogether. These techno-progressives are urging us to "transcend humanity" and embrace the next step in our evolution, which is, of course, to merge biology with technology, to alter and augment our minds and bodies and, in effect, become superhuman, ending disease (good) and even death— an alluring yet bizarre quest.

Interest in this notion of transhumanism is on the rise, and to me it is one of the most troubling developments I have observed in my 15 years of being a futurist. It is frankly a rather delusional idea to try and achieve human happiness by seeking to transcend humanity altogether through technological means.

For context, here are two contrasting positions on the concept, as laid out by transhumanism advocate and 2016 US Presidential Candidate Zoltan Istvan and the philosopher Jesse I. Bailey:

**The Protagonist.** Istvan writes in his 2013 novel *The Transhumanist Wager:*

> The bold code of the transhumanist will rise. That's an inevitable, undeniable fact. It's embedded in the undemocratic nature of technology and our own teleological evolutionary advancement. It is the future. We are the future, like it or not. And it needs to [be] molded, guided, and handled correctly by the strength and wisdom of transhumanist scientists with their nations and resources standing behind them, facilitating them. It needs to be supported in a way that we can make a successful transition into it, and not sacrifice ourselves—either by its overwhelming power or by a fear of harnessing that power.
>
> You need to put your resources into the technology. Into our education system. Into our universities, industries, and ideas. Into the strongest of our society. Into the brightest of our society. Into the best of our society. So that we can attain the future.[22]

**The Humanist.** Challenging this position, Bailey writes in *The Journal of Evolution and Technology:*

> I argue that by threatening to obscure death as a foundational possibility for *dasein* (human existence), transhumanism poses

the danger of hiding the need to develop a free and authentic relation to technology, Truth, and ultimately to *dasein* itself.

Transhumanists often make one of two claims: Either the body we inhabit now will be able to live for hundreds of years or our consciousness will be downloadable into multiple bodies. Either of these positions (in subtly, but importantly, different ways) alienates human experience from central aspects of the finitude of embodiment.

Heidegger locates being-toward-death as central to the call to authenticity, and away from lostness in the they-self (for whom technological enframing holds sway); by threatening our awareness of our own mortality, transhumanism thus threatens to occlude the call to authenticity, just as it occludes the need for it.[23]

It is clear that technological determinism is not the solution, and that the prevailing Silicon Valley ideology that argues, "Why don't we just invent our way out of this, have loads of fun, make lots of money while also improving the lives of billions of people with these amazing new technologies?" could prove to be just as lazy—and dangerous—as Luddism.

In respectful contrast to some transhumanists' rather Cartesian or reductionist views of humanity's future (i.e. vastly simplified and reduced to looking at the world—and people—as a giant machine), this book will strive to outline a mindset and Digital Age philosophy that I sometimes call exponential humanism. Through this philosophy, I believe we can find a balanced way forward that will allow us to embrace technology but not become technology, to use it as a tool and not as a purpose.

To safeguard humanity's future, we must invest as much energy in furthering humanity as we do in developing technology. I believe that if we want a world that remains a good place for humans, with all our imperfections and inefficiencies, we must put significant resources (monetary and otherwise) into defining what a new kind of exponential humanism may actually entail. It will not be enough to just invest into the technologies that promise to make us superhuman—as we will soon ride on the shoulders of machines whose workings we don't even understand any more.

If we don't become more proactive on these issues, I worry that an exponential, unfettered, and uncontrolled intelligence explosion in robotics, AI, bioengineering, and genetics will eventually lead to a systematic disregard of the basic principles of human existence, because technology does not have ethics—but a society without ethics is doomed.

This dichotomy is arising everywhere: Pretty much everything that can be digitized, automated, virtualized, and robotized probably will be, yet there are some things we should not attempt to digitize or automate—because they define what we are as humans.

This book explores where exponential and converging technologies might take us in the next ten years, highlights what is at stake, and explores what we can do about it today. No matter what your philosophical or religious persuasion, you will probably agree that technology has already entered our daily lives to such a vast degree that any further exponential progress will surely demand a new kind of conversation about where the advances are taking us, and why. Just as technology is literally about to enter our bodies and biological systems, it is time for a tribal pow-wow—the most important conversation the human tribe may ever have.

# Chapter 2
# Tech vs. Us

*Let's stop and consider our humanity for a moment.*

A human being's cognitive ability is, among many other things, based on our genetic dispositions and approximately 100 billion neurons in our brain.

If all were simultaneously improved by technology, simply in terms of performance or connectivity, it might soon be possible to achieve, very roughly, about 100 standard deviations of improvement. This would give the average human an IQ of over 1,000 compared to the average range of between 70 and 130 that covers roughly 95% of the population.[24]

It is hard to comprehend what capabilities that level of intelligence would represent, but it would surely be far beyond anything we have witnessed or could imagine. Cognitive engineering, via direct edits to embryonic human DNA, could eventually produce individuals whose cognitive ability exceeds even the most remarkable of human intellects throughout history. By 2050, this process will likely have begun. Revamping a machine's operating system is one thing, but what does it mean to reprogram a sentient being with memories and a sense of free will (assuming that this will still matter in 2050)?

Let's start by looking at what defines being human. Countless philosophers have struggled with this question, but now that we are reaching the point when technology is gearing up to allow us to augment, alter, reprogram, or even redesign humans, this is now a burning issue. Many voices in the Singularity and transhumanism camps are arguing that we are heading towards the merging of man and machine, of technology and biology. Exciting or not, if that will indeed be the case, defining humanity in the Digital Age will be even more essential.

### Ethics and values as human essences

The fundamental challenge here will be that while technology knows no ethics, norms, or beliefs, the effective functioning of every human and every society is entirely predicated upon them. Machines may eventually learn how to read or comprehend our societal or moral considerations and ethical quandaries, but will they have compassion or empathy, will they actually exist in a holistic way, as we do? In fact, we live life largely according to our values, beliefs, and mindsets, not according to data and algorithms. Even if machines can eventually analyze and possibly simulate how humans do this, they would still be a long way from existing as we do.

As I've said, we are at a pivot point on the exponential curve where the next step is a very big leap from four to eight and then sixteen. Hence, we are facing an enormous gap between what technology can do (the answer seems to be pretty much anything), and what it should do to result in overall human happiness. Indeed, when we go beyond the obvious causes of non-happiness such as lack of freedom, inequality, poverty, and disease, the answer to "what defines happiness?" is neither certain nor universally consistent (see chapter 9).

Clearly, apart from being able to simulate human interactions increasingly well, technology does not know nor does it care for happiness, self-realization, fulfillment, emotion, or values and beliefs. It only understands logic, rational action, (in)completion, efficiency, and yes/no answers because in order to "know happiness" you'd have to be able to actually be happy, which in my view requires embodiment.

Technology is entirely nihilistic about the things we humans truly care about. I believe it cannot and should not move up Maslow's hierarchy of needs pyramid from helping with basic needs towards love and belonging, self-esteem, or self-realization.[25] Yes, sure, neural networks and deep-learning approaches have recently made it possible for computers to teach themselves how to do complex things such as winning GO games, [26] and I guess it would—in theory—be possible for machines to teach themselves how to act like a human. Nevertheless, simulation is not the same as duplication; mediating reality is not the same as reality itself.

Technology has no ethics—and nor should it! At the same time, in this exponential age, human brains and bodies are increasingly being treated as machine-like objects, as a fancy wetware (a flesh and blood version of software) challenge. And we can only shiver to imagine what would happen if computers were programmed to emulate or even develop their own machine ethics or beliefs. In the author's opinion, it is not a path we should pursue. The idea of giving machines the ability to "be" might well qualify as a crime against humanity.

### Born and raised inside a machine?

As a rather jarring example, consider the increasingly discussed and controversial concept of ectogenesis—the idea of literally growing a baby outside a woman's body in an artificial womb.[27] This might become feasible in the next 15–20 years, and it makes a great example for how a technological "yes we can" attitude can override even the most basic of human considerations. While going about human reproduction in this futuristic manner might be less taxing for women than a pregnancy, more efficient, and ultimately probably cheaper, I believe it would also be utterly dehumanizing and detrimental for a baby to be born in such a way. I don't know about you, but I struggle to understand the rationale of those who develop and promote such concepts.

### Is this good for humanity? A basic test

In the face of exponential change and hence ever more challenging choices for humanity, I propose we devise a set of questions against which we can gauge new scientific and technological breakthroughs, for example:

- Does this idea violate the human rights of anyone involved?
- Does this idea seek to replace human relationships with machine relationships, or does it promote the concept?
- Does this idea put efficiency over humanity, does it seek to automate what should not be automated such as essential human interactions?
- Does this idea put traditional, GDP-centric thinking (profits and growth) over the most basic human ethics?
- Does it replace the human quest for happiness with mere consumption?
- Does this idea automate core human activities that should not be automated, for example, an automated cleric or an artificial intelligence (AI) therapist?

One of my favorite science fiction authors, William Gibson, once remarked, "Technologies are morally neutral until we apply them."[28] Indeed, his keen and often-quoted observation is extremely relevant for what is facing us at this precise moment, when the very definition of being human is increasingly impacted by exponential technological advances.

**The 90/10 challenge: at the pivot point**
Because we are at the hinge of the exponential curve, today, we have a unique chance to impact our future. Will it be 90% positive because of these technological advances, with the remaining 10% representing manageable risks and challenges? Or, will it run out of control, flip and spiral towards a dystopian 10/90 world?

Most technology developments are still largely positive in nature. Continued advances in battery and solar technologies represent a huge step in the global shift towards sustainability and renewable energy, and the latest Internet of Things (IoT) applications are enabling a veritable sea change in areas such as smart ports, smart cities, and smart farming.

Yet, while we are at 90% positive today, the still relatively minor negative consequences are now starting to mushroom quickly because not enough inventors, scientists, entrepreneurs, and other market participants are looking at addressing them. In the case of the IoT (see chapter 5), if done badly, without caution, this may well result in the biggest surveillance network and global panopticon ever built.[29] We may end up being observed, monitored, and tracked from every angle, all the time, anywhere, and by default, without control or recourse.

Exponential technologies have truly amazing potential for humanity, but we may squander it if we do not think holistically or forget that the purpose of all technology and business in general should be to promote human flourishing.

## Technology, power, and responsibility

Power comes with consequences—and right now we are busy enjoying the much increased powers of technology but often fail to act responsibly when it comes to the unintended consequences and resulting fundamental changes in the fabric of society.

We love to connect with each other and promote ourselves on Facebook, and many of us enjoy the tingle of every "like." Yet so far, this particular Faustian Bargain—social networks, where we trade our personal data for the free use of an exciting global platform—has not included holding companies such as Facebook truly responsible for what they do with all those digital breadcrumbs they have collected about us. And of course, Facebook is a master at shirking the issue because giving us more control over our data will certainly not help their monetization efforts, given that their underlying business model is to sell us to the highest bidder.

Facebook wants us to feel responsible for what we are doing while we revel in its powerful pleasure trap, and just like the National Rifle Association (NRA), it keeps pointing out that some people use technology for bad things, while technology companies themselves are not responsible. Akin to the NRA's "Guns don't kill people, people kill people" stance, I think this is just a really cheap way of denying responsibility for what they facilitate.

Similarly, we love using Google Maps, Google Now, and maybe even Google Home (a home device you can talk to just like a robotic servant), to anticipate traffic issues or send an update to our next appointments. However, we cannot seem to find a good way to hold Google responsible for mining and then selling our (albeit crudely anonymized) meta-data to marketing companies, or giving it to any government agency armed with a Foreign Intelligence Surveillance Act (FISA) rubber stamp. Very soon, it will be a certainty that most of us will use voice-controlled intelligent digital assistants (IDAs) on our mobile devices, yet it seems that nobody will be held accountable for what they will do behind the scenes. These devices will constantly listen to us, yet we have no control over them. We are indeed creating thinking machines without a responsible plan, and without oversight or recourse.

We are entering a world where automated, cloud-based intelligent agent software robots (bots) can carry out all kinds of tasks on behalf of their users, such as setting up meetings or booking restaurants. We will not even be able to comprehend how our bots have arrived at their decisions, and yet they will increasingly run our lives.

We are witnessing a general lack of foresight and caution around the use and impact of technology. This is primarily because responsibility for what technology makes possible is still largely considered an externality by those who create and sell it—and that is a totally unsustainable attitude towards the future. This reminds me of how, for the longest time, the oil companies got away with considering pollution and global warming an externality to their business, i.e. something that was not their responsibility. Needless to say, this kind of approach to our future is a bad idea, and it is likely ruinous.

I fundamentally believe we must urgently look beyond profit and growth when it is about technology that can dramatically alter human existence. This moral imperative surpasses even that of the nuclear age. To quote J. Robert Oppenheimer, one of the co-inventors of the nuclear bomb, following the Hiroshima and Nagasaki bombings: "Now I am become Death, the destroyer of worlds."[30] In quoting the Hindu scripture, the *Bhagavad-Gita*, Oppenheimer was signaling a whole new phase of human evolution. Right now, we are unconsciously experiencing something even larger.

> *"As I'll argue, AI is a dual-use technology like nuclear fission. Nuclear fission can illuminate cities or incinerate them. Its terrible power was unimaginable to most people before 1945. With advanced AI, we're in the 1930s right now. We're unlikely to survive an introduction as abrupt as nuclear fission's."* –James Barrat, Our Final Invention: Artificial Intelligence and the End of the Human Era[31]

## Technology is not what we seek, but how we seek

Technology, no matter how magical, is simply a tool that we use to achieve something: Technology is not what we seek, but how we seek! The word technology stems from the Greek root *techne*, which refers to "the bringing forth of the true into the beautiful," and to the improvement in skills of craftsmen and artists via the use of such tools.[32] The Greek philosophers also saw technology very much as something that is an innate human activity—we invent and improve tools all the time and it is human nature to do so.

Today, however, we are heading into a future where a stunning reversal of that tool-intent is starting to happen: Philosopher and intellectual Herbert Marshall McLuhan once suggested that the tools we make are starting to shape us, or even invent us.[33] Taken to the exponential extremes, this will be a perversion of the original intent of *techne*—and we would get to play God for only a very short time!

Sure, you may argue that technology has always impacted and changed humanity, so what's new, what's there to worry about? Isn't this just another instance of the same *techne* flow?

Let's consider that technology in its original *techne* meaning was merely a tool for enhancing our capabilities and our performances, our productivity, our reach, and our possibilities. We see this in inventions such as the steam engine, the telephone, the car, and the Internet. Technology did not enhance us in our entirety, only our actions and outward possibilities. None of these technological advancements changed us inside, materially, as humans in a deeply and irreversibly neurological, biological, or even psychological or spiritual way. Using those technologies was not really making us exponentially more powerful, at least not in the sense of being at the pivot point of the exponential curve.

While the invention of the steam engine did make a huge difference during the Industrial Age, it was still very early as far as the exponential curve is concerned. In contrast, the advent of advanced robotics and the resulting widespread automation of labor are now happening during the inflection point on that scale (four)—and therein lies the difference. It is a difference in order of magnitude, not just in style but in kind.

### Algorithms vs. Androrithms

Being human is largely about those things that we cannot—for the foreseeable future—compute, measure, algorithmically define, simulate, or completely understand. What makes us human is not mathematical or even just chemical or biological. It involves those things that are largely unnoticed, unsaid, subconscious, ephemeral, and unobjectifiable. These are the human essences that I like to call androrithms that we absolutely must keep even if they appear to be clumsy, complicated, slow, risky, or inefficient compared to nonbiological systems, computers, and robots.

We should not attempt to mend, fix, upgrade, or even eradicate what makes us human; rather, we should design technology to know and respect these differences—and protect them. Unfortunately, the slow but systematic reduction or even discarding of androrithms—those elusive traits that make us human—has already started all around us. For example, social networks allow us to create our own profiles as we see fit, and revel in our fabricated identities, rather than wrestle with the one we actually have in real life, aka in our meatspace.

That might appear good but could become very negative if taken too far. While of course there are overlaps between our social-network and real-life identities, the face-to-face, embodied socializing quality of androrithms is now increasingly replaced with artful screens and clever algorithms, such as for online content curation and matchmaking. There, we can shape ourselves any way we want, using mostly free yet powerful technologies, and soon we begin to think of ourselves as what philosopher Dr. Jesse Bailey describes as "technological products of our own rational calculative control."[34] Unsurprisingly, an increasing number of people feel very lonely, and even depressed, on social networks.[35]

The often brilliant—if somewhat politically derailed —German philosopher Martin Heidegger stated in his book *Sein und Zeit* (*Being and Time*) that "a human being is the only entity which in its existence has this very Being as an issue."[36] The German word *dasein* (being there) really describes it best.

*Dasein* speaks to the core of the difference between (wo)man and machine and is an important theme throughout this book: It is the sentient being that is at the core of our human desires—the mind, the spirit, or the soul, that elusive part of us that we cannot seem to define or even locate, but that nevertheless runs our lives.

## STEM and CORE

The bottom line is that the magnitude of human mysteries—the interplay of body and mind, of biology and spirituality, that which is not rational, not computable, not copyable, not engineerable—still massively dwarfs the scope of science, technology, engineering, and mathematics (STEM). We should, therefore, not anthropomorphize our technologies too much, or confuse our priorities when it comes to making important societal choices and decisions, and we should not forget our responsibility as we venture out to create technology that may end up surpassing us.

As much as I am enthralled by STEM breakthroughs, I believe that we urgently need to create a counterbalance, one that amplifies the importance of truly human factors. In contrast to the STEM acronym, I have recently started calling this CORE: creativity/compassion, originality, reciprocity/responsibility, and empathy.

The immediate concern is not so much humanity's potential annihilation by machines, but rather our being lured into technology's amazing wormholes, virtual worlds, and simulations in a manner that first diminishes and then demolishes those very things that make us human.

### Could we end up developing a preference for technology over humanity?

For the present and the foreseeable future, even our greatest technologies will still only be able to simulate being human (*dasein*) in some way or other, rather than actually becoming human. Therefore, for the time being, the key challenge is not so much about technology replacing humanity or even annihilating it, but whether we may start preferring really great simulations—cheaply and skillfully provided by machines—to our actual, embodied reality. In other words, will we eventually prefer relationships with machines rather than with people?[37]

Will we soon be content with having conversations with our digital assistants, eating 3D printed food, traveling instantly to virtual worlds, ordering personalized on-demand services delivered to our smart homes by drones or via the cloud, and literally being serviced by robots?[38]

Will very high convenience, very low prices, ease of use (soon to be achieved completely, no doubt), and humanity's rather high aptitude for laziness win over our need for "wetware" interactions and actual experiences? That may be hard to imagine today, but it could become exceedingly likely in less than ten years. Maybe "What if?" has already become "What then?"

We are already seeing technologies such as augmented reality (AR) and virtual reality (VR), holograms, and brain-computer interfaces (BCI) making it much easier to augment or simulate realities that used to be "human-senses-only" experiences, gradually then suddenly increasing the likelihood that we will start confusing one with the other.

## Interfaces and ethics

I predict that, in just a few years, using AR and VR will become as normal as sending messages or communicating via apps today. Just imagine what happens to the way we'll see the world if hundreds of millions of people start using these devices. Would it be human to be constantly augmented in this way? Who will be responsible for defining the principles of augmentation of human senses—for example, would it be legal (or ethical, for that matter) to view an artificially simulated sexual image of a person overlaid on their actual body as we are talking to them? Could you be fired for refusing to work in VR worlds? Or even worse, would you ever want to return to a world without AR/VR once it becomes so immersive and ubiquitously available?

And last but not least: Who will be our stewards in this coming era of sensual augmentation by AR and VR? Virtual travel technologies such as Facebook's Oculus Rift, Samsung VR, and Microsoft's HoloLens are just beginning to provide us with a very real feeling for what it would be like to raft the Amazon River or climb Mount Fuji. These are already very interesting experiences that will certainly change our way of experiencing reality, of communicating, of working, and of learning. But can we or should we prevent the future experience providers from always presenting only "doctored" versions of reality—for example, cleaning up the slums of Mumbai every time we drive by in a taxi?

Will we still be human if we start preferring to always experience the world like this? Is there anything we can do to prevent AR/VR from becoming standard tools for society just like mobile devices and social networks? Could we propose to use them in moderation, like some kind of souped-up TV, or would we be tempted to think of the regular, un-augmented world as boring? Consider how many kids today think of going to a beach without Wi-Fi as a real drag. These are dilemmas, indeed, and they will not be solved by simple yes-or-no answers. A balanced, situational, and human-centric approach will be required.

Let us consider that there is still a huge difference between these new ways to experience alternate realities and real life. Picture yourself standing in the middle of a crowded bazaar in Mumbai, India, for just two minutes. Then, compare the memories you would have accumulated in a very short time with those from a much longer but simulated experience using the most advanced systems available today or in the near future. The smells, the sounds and sights, your body's reactions, the general onslaught on your senses . . . all of these are a thousand times more intense than what even the most advanced gadgetry, fueled by exponential technological gains, could ever hope to simulate.

This is the difference between a holistic, embodied, contextual, and complete human experience and a machine-generated simulation. Yet, a great simulation is no bad thing—as long as we know what it is, and if it does not tempt us into "preferring it over us" we can probably use most of it for good purposes.

Visual technologies are bound to become almost infinitely better in the very near future, hugely upping the ante and further blurring human/machine boundaries over time. Once we can literally step into the scene of a movie with VR, the capabilities of our own minds and imagination might be surpassed forever.[39] And that is exactly what both excites and deeply worries me. Are we meant to do this? Are we wired for this kind of virtuality? Will our wiring need to change as a result, and how would we go about that? Do we need new, nonbiological wires to make this work?

No matter how we answer these questions, if and when exponential technological progress means that our bodies will no longer be central to our identity, we will have crossed the threshold to becoming like machines. Would it lessen our humanity if our biological computing capabilities need constant upgrades to remain useful? By then, we could well have given up 95% of our potential in favor of "becoming the tools we have created."[40]

### Artificial intelligence and the blurring of human boundaries

Given the scale of its potential impact, we should consider the role of AI in this blurring of the human-machine distinction. Consider DeepMind, a leading AI firm in London, acquired by Google in 2015.

In a February 2016 interview with *The Guardian*, DeepMind's CEO, Demis Hassabis, highlighted AI's potential:

> There's such an information overload that it's becoming difficult for even the smartest humans to master it in their lifetimes. How do we sift through this deluge of data to find the right insights? One way of thinking of artificial general intelligence is as a process that will automatically convert unstructured information into actionable knowledge. What we're working on is potentially a meta-solution to any problem.[41]

What could this grand statement mean in practice? Imagine a society where technology—particularly AI—provides the meta-solutions to any of society's perceived grand challenges, from diseases, aging and death, to climate change, global warming, energy production, food production, and even terrorism. Imagine a machine intelligence that could easily compute more information than we could ever hope to comprehend, a machine that would literally read the entire world's data in real time, all the time, anywhere. This machine (and those that own or run it) would become a kind of global brain, unimaginably powerful, beyond human understanding. Is that where companies like DeepMind and Google want to take us, and if so, how could we possibly retain our human qualities in that scenario?

> *"The attribution of intelligence to machines, crowds of fragments, or other nerd deities obscures more than it illuminates. When people are told that a computer is intelligent, they become prone to changing themselves in order to make the computer appear to work better, instead of demanding that the computer be changed to become more useful." –Jaron Lanier,* You Are Not a Gadget[42]

### Can technology grasp what really matters?
Let's imagine that such a machine, an AI-in-the-cloud, were to exist (and in reality we are not that far away from the first editions). Would it actually read, understand, or appreciate those interactions between

humans that are not expressed as data? Could it understand *dasein*, being?

Despite the exponential technological gains that are certain to happen, the human way of being and of experiencing things remains dramatically different from how technologies capture those very same moments that matter to us. Even the best photographs, videos, or data trails are just mere approximations of what it was like to have actually been there—it is the context, the embodiment, the completeness of that unique moment that somehow resides in us.

Some philosophers have argued that we can never actually capture, retain, or reproduce what really matters. If that is true, how could we ever hope to capture some kind of simulated humanness inside of a machine? Would we not incur a very high risk of losing 95% of what makes us human if we were to "go beyond the limitations of biology" as the transhumanist movement is suggesting?

Wikipedia defines transhumanism as:

> ...an international and intellectual movement that aims to transform the human condition by developing and creating widely available sophisticated technologies to greatly enhance human intellectual, physical, and psychological capacities.[43]

This ominous promise of "great enhancement" is exactly what worries me most about transhumanism. As enticing as it may be to enhance my capacities, it seems to me that those very same businesses, platforms, and technologies that provide the necessary means of enhancement are also the ones that will benefit the most from this concept. These companies will indeed be much enhanced in their power, reach, and market value, while ordinary humans will increasingly struggle to keep up with their enhanced siblings. The business of replacing androrithmic, intrinsically human experiences with algorithms, software, and AI that promise godlike power will, of course, be huge—but is that in itself a plus? Should we leave our future to those who want to turn it into a giant cloud operating system (OS) because it makes boatloads of money?

> *"What I'm saying now is we are as gods and*
> *have to get good at it." –Stewart Brand*[44]

As a case in point, many transhumanist evangelists are quick to point out that humans are really just wetware that need some serious fixing and upgrading. They contend that we aren't smart enough, fast enough, big enough, or agile enough. Humans, they argue, will simply require software and hardware upgrades, mostly because doing so will bring about the end of aging, and possibly even the end of death.

Is turning ourselves into machines, partly or completely, simply the next logical step in our evolution? Are we destined to leave our biological limitations behind and augment ourselves with technology?

The concept of likening living beings to machines is not new; the great philosopher and rationalist René Descartes already likened animals to very complex automatons in the 16th century.[45] Today, many technologists are reviving this concept, which I like to call machine thinking, by proposing that everything around us—and within us—can be thought of as an apparatus that can be altered, fixed, and duplicated. To them, human existence, in the end, is nothing but very fancy science.

For example, medicating ourselves to lower our cholesterol or blood pressure, or to avoid pregnancy, already represent significant but widely accepted intrusions into the body's natural workings. Yet the next few steps in medical innovation could take the impact to another level of magnitude altogether. Examples might include implanting nonbiological components within human bodies (such as nanobots in our bloodstream taking care of our cholesterol problem), altering our very genes to avoid diseases (or to program our babies), or implanting cognitive stimulation devices into our brains to increase our performance.

Is this simply our inescapable evolution, or is it a bizarre quest for superhuman power that defies our very nature, design, and purpose? Is humanity really destined to recreate and program itself, to have limitless options as to what we can be, to never die, to . . . become as god? Even if you are not religious (and just to clarify, I certainly am not) this question goes to the core of the matter.

Increased human happiness and global, collective flourishing will not result from becoming more like a machine, even if that could actually provide some kind of superpower (which it won't, anytime soon). Rather, I argue that we should challenge the core premises of transhumanism (such as the idea of going beyond our biological limitations) instead of accepting them as inevitable.

It is also important to realize and accept that our humanity is actually something we must and should wrestle with; it is something we have to guard and work hard to keep. Meaningful relationships are often the result of struggles and conflicts, and love is never sustained by simply letting it happen. Being human is not something that we can—or should—just consume by buying some fancy technology. There is no app for that.

What would a future feel like that carves a path between the transhumanists and the exponential humanitarians like myself? Is there a middle way between technology and humanity, and what could it look like?

I think there is, and I am on a mission to define it.

# Chapter 3
# The Megashifts

*Technological shifts are rewiring society and transforming the landscape.*

I believe the coming clash between man and machine will be intensified and exponentalized through the combinatorial effects of ten great shifts—Megashifts, if you will, namely:

1. Digitization
2. Mobilization
3. Screenification
4. Disintermediation
5. Transformation
6. Intelligization
7. Automation
8. Virtualization
9. Anticipation
10. Robotization

As a paradigm change is to thinking and philosophy, so a Megashift represents a huge evolutionary step for society, one that may seem gradual at first . . . but then has a very sudden impact. Below I explore the nature of these Megashifts and then go on to describe each of them and their potential implications.

### Exponential and simultaneous

Many of the world's great innovations were born decades, sometimes centuries, before they eventually swept through human society. They often occurred in a relatively sequential manner, each following and building on the previous ones. In contrast, Megashifts might grow slowly as well but many were born together. They have now started sweeping through society simultaneously and at a much faster pace.

Megashifts present immediate and complex challenges and differ in nature to the forces that have swept through society and business in the past. A key difference here is that a relatively few organizations and individuals that anticipate and find ways of exploiting or addressing a Megashift can normally expect to find opportunities and reap the biggest benefits. You may be familiar with these terms already, but now I want you to imagine them as distinct technological forces combining to create a perfect storm for humanity. Technostress? The challenges we have experienced so far won't even register on the stress scale when compared with what's to come…

### Megashift 1: Digitization

Everything that can be digitized, will be. The first wave included music, then movies and TV, then books and newspapers. Now it is impacting money, banking, insurance, healthcare, pharmaceuticals, transportation, cars, and cities. Soon it will have transformational impact in logistics, shipping, manufacturing, food, and energy. It is important to note that when something gets digitized and moved to the cloud, it often becomes free or at least vastly cheaper. Consider what happened with Spotify: In Europe an individual 12-song CD used to cost around €20 (US$22)—and now you can get 16 million songs for €8 (US$9) per month, or listen to them free on YouTube.

While I am a happy and faithful Spotify subscriber and enjoy it very much, this kind of margin-destroying Digital Darwinism brings a huge shift in business models and forces most incumbents to transform or perish. In my 2005 book *The Future of Music* (Berklee Press), I discussed at length what seems to me a certainty—that the big record labels that controlled the music industry for decades will cease to exist because distributing music is no longer a viable business.[46]

Indeed, Sir Paul McCartney has famously compared incumbent record labels to dinosaurs wondering what happened after the asteroid.[47] While that is an accurate image of the "psychic whiplash" being experienced by the established rulers of this once lucrative kingdom, it gives no indication of the speed of extinction. Crocodiles survived and some dinosaurs evolved into chickens—but digital Megashifts pay little homage to history and take no prisoners.

In 2010, I coined the phrase "the people formerly known as consumers"; for them, digitization often means cheaper goods and widely improved availability.[48] That's generally a positive, but then again, cheaper goods can also mean fewer jobs and lower wages. Witness the digitization of mobility with Uber and its rivals around the world like Lyft, Gett, and Ola Cabs in India. We can now order a taxi ride using an app on our smartphone, and it will often be cheaper than the incumbent competition. But will this economy work for the taxi drivers in the long term, or are we heading into a Darwinian "gig economy," a situation where we all work a multitude of relatively poorly paid freelance gigs rather than regular jobs?[49]

Regardless of societal challenges, the rapid digitization, automation, and virtualization of our world are probably inevitable. In practice, the rate may sometimes be constrained by fundamental laws of physics such as the hereto unmet energy needs of supercomputers or the minimum viable size of a computer chip—often cited as the reason why Moore's Law will not prevail forever.

This assumption of continued and pervasive penetration of technology points towards a future where what cannot be digitized and/or automated (see Automating Society, chapter 4) could become extremely valuable. As discussed in chapter 2, these androrithms capture essential human qualities such as emotions, compassion, ethics, happiness, and creativity.

While algorithms, software, and artificial intelligence (AI) will increasingly "eat the world" (as venture capitalist Marc Andreessen likes to say),[50] we must place the same value on androrithms—those things which make us uniquely human.

As previously expensive products and services become cheap and abundant, androrithms must take center stage with technology if we are to remain a society that is concerned with human flourishing. We certainly would not want to go from software eating the world to software cheating the world!

For example, I foresee that in the near future we will see a shift in how organizations look at business metrics such as Key Performance Indicators (KPI)—a term widely used in business goal setting and human resources. Our future KPIs may no longer be built merely on counting and qualifying our professional achievements based on quantifiable facts and data such as unit sales, customer contacts, satisfaction ratings, or lead conversion ratios. Instead, we may see the rise of what I call Key Human Indicators, which will reflect a much more holistic and ecosystemic approach to gauging people's contributions. It is not the quantified employee but the qualified human that we should be pursuing!

As with all the Megashifts, digitization is both a blessing and a curse and, either way, it is not something we can just switch off or delay significantly—therefore, it is imperative that we prepare accordingly.

**Megashift 2: Mobilization and mediazation**
Computing is no longer something we do mostly on computers, and by 2020 even the idea will seem utterly fossilized. Computing has become invisible and ingrained into our lives, piggybacking on what we used to call mobile telephones. Connectivity is the new oxygen, while computing is the new water. Both next-to-limitless connectivity and computational capability will become the new normal.

Music is mobile, movies are mobile, books are mobile, banking is mobile, maps are mobile . . . the list keeps growing. Mobilization also means that technology is moving much closer to (and soon, into) us—from the desktop into my hand or onto my wrist via wearable devices such as watches, then onto my face as augmented reality (AR) or virtual reality (VR) glasses or contact lenses, and soon directly in to my brain through brain–computer interfaces (BCI) or implants. As Gartner suggests, sync me, know me, track me, see me, hear me, understand me . . . be me—that's where mobilization is taking us.[51]

> *"There will come a time when it isn't 'They're spying on me through my phone' anymore. Eventually, it will be 'My phone is spying on me.'"* –Philip K. Dick[52]

Cisco predicts that by 2020, almost 80% of the world's Internet traffic will come via mobile devices, which will handle almost everything that used to be done only on desktops.[53] That is already the case when looking at roles as diverse as graphic designers, telecom engineers, and logistics service planners and providers. And much of it will be done by voice, touch, gesture, or AI—no more typing!

The rapid rise of digitization and mobilization has also resulted in the mediazation (recording) of everything as well as the datafication of information, where things once held in analog form as non-data—such as medical information shared in conversation with my doctor —have migrated onto the cloud as electronic records. Much of what used to be shared and experienced without much use of technology, in actual person-to-person interactions, is now being captured, filtered, or transmitted on smart devices with powerful screens.

Images and memories that we historically stored only in our biological hippocampus are now routinely vacuumed up by mobile devices and shared online at a rate of over two billion images per day.[54] Deloitte Global projects that, collectively, people will share over one trillion images online in 2016.[55]

News that used to be printed is now streamed through apps, becoming liquid and malleable. Social dating that used to get started in cafes and bars is now facilitated through a few swipes on an app. Restaurants that used to be discovered through the private recommendations of good friends are now identified through online rating engines that provide user reviews and websites offering 360° views of their kitchens (and the food!). Medical advice used to require local nurses and doctors—now it is delivered via devices that promise a better medical diagnosis right from your home for a fraction of the cost. Scanadu is a remote diagnosis device that measures your vitals—including your blood—and connects to the cloud for an instant analysis.[56] Many experiences that used to arrive through person-to-person communications are now becoming media.

The bottom line is everything that can be mobilized probably will be, but not every mobilized experience should be media-ized as a consequence.

We must consider the possibility that the prevailing technological imperative of "doing it because we can" may no longer be a clever move. Exponential technological advances will enable us to do much larger and more complex tasks, including activities that will have material impact on our behavior and our experiences as humans—and not always in a positive manner.

Consider, for example, the previously unrealistic possibility of tracking every single person who uses the Internet via their mobile gadgets. Yes, our "always on" devices have the benefits of total connectivity and constant activity monitoring via our health-tracking apps and step-counting devices. However, we will also become exceedingly trackable, naked, predictable, manipulated, and ultimately . . . programmable.

Here are some critical questions we should ask ourselves when determining the extent to which we want technology to intervene in our human experiences:

- Do we really need to photograph or record everything around us in order to create a complete "machine in the cloud" memory of our lives?
- Do we really need to share every aspect of our lives on digital platforms and social networks? Does that make us look (and feel) more like machines or more like humans?
- Do we really need to rely on live, real-time translation apps such as SayHi or Microsoft Translate to converse with someone in another language? Admittedly that can be quite useful when in a tight spot, but it also puts yet another media/device barrier between us and other people; it media-izes a uniquely human

process. Here again, it is about a new balance we will need to strike, not just about a yes/no answer.

## Megashift 3: Screenification and interface (r)evolutions

From type to touch and talk, almost everything that used to be consumed as print on paper is now migrating to a screen. These interface (r)evolutions mean that newspapers are very likely not going to be read on paper at all within just ten years. The same fate, no doubt, will overtake magazines, but somewhat more slowly, because most magazines are also about the sensations of touch and scent. They are just more experiential in the raw that way.

Paper maps are already moving to devices and will likely disappear almost completely in a few short years. Banking used to be done in buildings or at automated teller machines; now it is going mobile and into the cloud at a frantic pace. Phone calls used to be made with telephones; now they are becoming video calls conducted via screen services like Skype, Google Hangouts, and FaceTime.

Robots used to have buttons or remote controls as interfaces; now it's all about screens that are made to look like faces—and we just talk to them. Cars used to have switches, buttons, simple displays, or custom consoles; now car controls are fully-fledged touchscreens. And the list doesn't just go on—it's about to explode!

As even more powerful visual augmentation devices flood into the market, our eyes are also being screenified. Even though there are already people suggesting we should upgrade them with technology, in the near future, we will still see with our own Human 1.0 eyes. However, many of us may also use augmented eyeglasses, Internet-enabled contact lenses, or visors that dramatically enhance what we see and how we can respond to it. The way we see the world is about to change, forever—a true HellVen situation.

Screenfication is a key trend in the convergence of human and machine and the growing debate over how far we should go with it. It paves the way towards widespread use of AR/VR and holograms.

We will have screens for everything, everywhere, and those screens, powered by solar energy and low cost, long-lasting batteries, may well become cheaper than fancy wallpaper. Hence, it will be very easy to take the next step and use screens as overlays of our actual reality—to present information or other contextual images on top of what we actually see around us. Within ten years, I would venture that using AR and VR will become as normal as using WhatsApp is today. That is both an exhilarating and a scary thought: At that point, who is to say what is real and what is not?

Consider what that will do to our self-perception as human beings. Imagine attaining such "super-vision" and visual omnipotence just by wearing Microsoft's US$250 HoloLens visor. Imagine a doctor wearing a Samsung VR headset during the next surgery and lessening the risk of malpractice suits just because she has better access to live data.

The world we see might become infinitely richer, faster, and more interconnected—but how disorienting and addictive could that be? And why would one ever want to see anything without those new super-enhancers? This will become even more of an issue as the suppliers of these products inevitably deploy armies of neuroscientists and behavioral experts to tell them how to make our screens even more addictive and convenient. If you think a Facebook "like" already gets your dopamine going, then how much deeper could the visual high become?

> *"Here though, there are no oppressors. No one's forcing you to do this. You willingly tie yourself to these leashes. And you willingly become utterly socially autistic. You no longer pick up on basic human communication cues. You're at a table with three humans, all of whom are looking at you and trying to talk to you, and you're staring at a screen! Searching for strangers in . . . Dubai!" –Dave Eggers, The Circle[57]*

## Megashift 4: Disintermediation

A key trend in online commerce, media, and communication is to cut out the middle man or woman—disruption by going direct. This has already happened in digital music, where the newer platforms like Apple, Spotify, Tencent, Baidu, and YouTube are disrupting and dislodging the record-label cartels that used to get 90% of an artist's earnings.

It's happening with tourism and hotels: Airbnb enables us to stay in private residences and book directly with the apartment owners, without the need for a traditional hotel.

It's happened in book publishing, where authors can now go direct with Amazon Kindle Publishing, getting up to 70% of the revenues on an eBook rather than 10% from a traditional publisher. Can you imagine the impact on the popularity and earnings of Tolstoy if he'd had that kind of direct access?

It's happening in banking transactions, where customers can now use tools like PayPal, M-Pesa in Africa, Facebook Money, and TransferWise to send payments around the globe. These services often bypass the banks and traditional money transfer services and the outrageous fees they presume to charge. Add retail, insurance, and soon energy to the equation and you can see where this is going: If it can be done direct and/or peer-to-peer, it will be. Technology is making it a certainty.

The key challenge is this: Disruption is great, disruption is exciting, disruption can be very lucrative—as evidenced by the much-hyped stories of startups achieving billion-dollar plus valuations in just a few years—but ultimately we also need construction.[58] On the surface, it seems fine to aim to join the ranks of firms with a valuation of US$1 billion (unicorn) or US$10 billion (decacorn). However, we need to go deeper to ensure we build something that creates a new and better infrastructure, as well as a societal context, not just something that has a high market capitalization, but adds nothing and simply takes away what used to be there.

Uber has disintermediated the taxi and limousine market, and that has been an amazing benefit to a lot of customers, as well as to the drivers and other Uber workers. However, in the process of becoming a very large and powerful player on this turf, Uber itself has become a new kind of intermediary. Some pundits are calling this "platform capitalism" and "digital feudalism" because of the way

Uber is treating its drivers as highly expendable commodities—a clear downside of the gig economy.[59]

The Uber example shows that it will not be enough to simply take apart what is no longer working so well, such as the taxi industry, or to reboot services where current market incumbents just don't care enough anymore. It is also necessary to build a complete, new digitally native ecosystem that will take care of all pieces of the puzzle, not just some of them. Skimming the cream off the top after disrupting outmoded business models is not sustainable. It's not just about disruption. It's also about construction.

Disintermediation is clearly driven by the power of exponential technologies, and we will see a lot more of that. The biggest tsunamis of change will be in health and energy. It will be essential to remember that mere disruption will not work and will not last. We also need to build true human values and a holistic ecosystem that generates lasting value for everyone; not just more algorithms but also replenished androrithms. We must take a holistic view to really make a difference.

> *"Before you become too entranced with gorgeous gadgets and mesmerizing video displays, let me remind you that information is not knowledge, knowledge is not wisdom, and wisdom is not foresight. Each grows out of the other, and we need them all." –Arthur C. Clarke*[60]

**Megashift 5: Transformation**
Going beyond mere change, the biggest meme in 2015 was "digital transformation," a phrase that has already acquired the somewhat stale taste of "social media." Nevertheless, the term is a good fit as it goes far beyond mere change or innovation. It literally means becoming something else, morphing from a caterpillar to a butterfly, or from a toy car to a toy robot, or indeed from a car manufacturer to a mobility provider. Transformation will be the number one priority for most companies and organizations as exponential technological change impacts them across the board. Transforming into what will

work five years from now requires a lot of foresight as well as courage, and naturally the support of all stakeholders and the capital markets.

But let's not forget that the mother of all transformations will be our own Megashift from being physically separate to being directly connected to computers and devices.

## Megashift 6: Intelligization

This is a core reason why humanity is being challenged as deeply as it is: Things are becoming intelligent.

Every object around us that used to be disconnected and without dynamic context is now being connected to the Internet via sensor networks and continuously updated and interrogated via global device grids.

Whatever can be made intelligent will be because now we have the means.

Deep learning is a key enabler of intelligization, and it is a huge game changer. Rather than using the traditional approach of programming machines to follow instructions and get a job done, the emerging dominant paradigm is to give them nothing but massive processing power, access to huge amounts of legacy and real-time data, a base set of learning rules, and a simple command such as, "Figure out how to win every single GO, chess, or backgammon game." The machine then comes up with rules and strategies that we humans might never discover ourselves.

Google's DeepMind AI labs demonstrated the power of deep learning in 2015 by showing that a computer can actually learn how to play and win Atari computer games entirely by itself, and then evolve to total mastery in a very short time.[61]

Shortly after the Atari demonstration, DeepMind developed AlphaGo—a self-learning computer that mastered the ancient and infinitely more difficult Chinese game of Go.[62] This is the holy grail of computer intelligence: Not the mathematical perfection that Deep Blue showed when it beat Gary Kasparov in chess,[63] but the capability for the machine to understand its surroundings and devise the best course of action itself—and recursively so. By repeatedly applying the same process, these AIs may become exponentially better, very quickly.

### Megashift 7: Automation

The great promise of many exponential technologies is that we can digitize everything, make it intelligent, and then automate and virtualize it. Automation is key to this idea of hyper-efficiency because it makes it possible to substitute humans with machines. I will address this Megashift in chapter 4 on the automation of society.

### Megashift 8: Virtualization

Virtualization, simply put, is the idea of creating a nonphysical, digital version of something, rather than having a tangible copy of it on location. Some of the most commonly used virtual services are desktop or server virtualization, where my workstation is in the cloud and only accessed through a terminal on my desk or an app on my smartphone. Another example is communications and networking: Rather than using networking hardware such as routers and switches, calls and data communications are increasingly routed in the cloud using software-defined networking (SDN). The resulting benefits include potentially huge cost savings and faster service, but it is also disrupting the business models of huge global players such as Cisco.

Virtualization via cloud computing can, some suggest, deliver up to 90% cost savings.[64] Rather than shipping printed books around the globe, Amazon virtualizes the bookstore and sends digital files to readers on their Kindle reader. We are already on the verge of virtualizing shipping, too. Imagine the savings from a 3D printer that can produce your iPhone cover right in your living room; you just need to download the design. Imagine a future 3D printer that can print even the most advanced products with hundreds of composite materials, right there in your favorite mall, producing anything from tennis shoes to Barbie dolls to a myriad of products.

Decentralization is often a major component of virtualization because we do not need a central distribution point if a product can be provided in the cloud. SDN systems do not need all the cables to run to a certain switch or box; all switching can be done remotely, allowing for significant savings. Naturally, security becomes a big issue when virtualizing or decentralizing assets because there are many fewer points of physical control.[65] That is a huge opportunity for innovative companies, but also a serious challenge for governments and politicians. How will we agree on the rules of engagement and the digital ethics behind the solutions to these technical challenges?

In the near future, virtualization will spread to all sectors such as banking, financial services, healthcare and pharmaceuticals—particularly in drug development. Digital therapeutics will aim to complement or even replace traditional medication by effecting behavioral modifications to reduce or even solve the same problem. Another powerful instance is cloud biology, where software ingests lab results and merges them with other data to help speed up the discovery of new drugs.

Now, imagine the exponential effect of combining the other Megashifts with virtualization. Virtualized cloud robots could make just about every process so much faster and more reliable, just as digitizing behavioral change may become an alternative to drugs.[66]

Needless to say, virtualization will be a driving force in the conflict between technology and humanity, including the loss of jobs, the likelihood that "software will soon eat biology," and the increasing temptation to virtualize humans via brain-uploading or cyborgism—the dream of many transhumanists.[67]

## Megashift 9: Anticipation

Computers are already becoming very good at anticipating our needs before we ourselves realize what they may be. Google Now and Google Home are intelligent digital assistants (IDAs) from Google, and a big part of the company's huge bet on AI. They will anticipate any changes in your daily schedule—be it airline delays, traffic, or meetings that overrun—and use the information to notify the next meeting about your delay, or even rebook a flight for you.[68]

Crime prevention based on algorithms is quickly becoming a very popular topic among law enforcement officials. These programs are essentially using big data such as crime statistics, social media, mobile phone locations, and traffic data to predict where a crime may happen so that police patrols in that area can be stepped up. In some cases, eerily reminding us of the "precogs" from *Minority Report*,[69] individuals have even been singled out for a visit by a social worker or a police official because the system indicated that they were very likely to commit a crime.

Imagine where this could go once the Internet of Things (IoT) rolls out globally, with sensor networks connecting hundreds of billions of objects such as traffic lights, cars, and environmental monitors. Imagine the anticipatory, predictive potential once we have AI tools to make sense out of all that data. In drug discovery, an AI tool running on a quantum computer could map out trillions of molecular combinations and instantly identify those that may work for a given treatment, or even help prevent the onset of a disease to begin with.

Imagine what could happen once notes and coins have gone digital, and every tiny purchase is trackable instantly—vastly more efficient yet also vastly more invasive. Lucrative digital transformations or Brave New World?

Despite the tantalizing promises that anticipatory technologies seem to offer, I see a number of vexing ethical issues emerging very quickly—key among them being:

- **Dependency** – Leaving our thinking to software and algorithms because it's just so much more convenient and fast.
- **Confusion** – Not knowing if it was the intended human who replied to my emails, or her AI assistant. Or even not knowing if I made my own decision or if I was manipulated by my IDA.
- **Loss of control** – Not having a way of knowing if the AI's anticipation was correct or not, as we could not possibly track the system's logic or even comprehend the workings of a quantum computing-fueled, machine-learning system. In other words, we would need to either trust it completely or not at all, similar to the dilemma that some airplane pilots are already facing with their autopilot systems.

- **Abdication** – Being tempted to leave more tasks to systems that would handle them for us, whether it is coordinating personal schedules, making appointments, or answering simple emails. Then, of course, it would be very likely that we would simply blame the cloud/bot/AI if something went wrong.

## Megashift 10: Robotization

Robots are the embodiment of all these Megashifts, where everything is converging in some spectacular new creations—and they are going to be absolutely everywhere, like it or not. As science makes big leaps in natural language understanding, image recognition, battery power, and new materials that allow better movement skills, we can expect the price of robots to fall dramatically while their usefulness—as well as their likeability—will skyrocket. Some robots might even be 3D printed, just as the first cars are now being manufactured almost entirely with 3D printers.[70]

The bottom line is that, as we head into exponential change, we must also collaborate to address ethics, culture, and values. Otherwise, it is certain that technology will gradually then suddenly become the purpose of our lives, rather than the tool to discover the purpose.

# Chapter 4
# Automating Society

*Higher productivity, better margins but fewer jobs, more techno-billionaires but a shrinking middle class?*

Of all the Megashifts, automation merits particular attention. Automation has been a strong driver of change throughout history, for example when hand-operated looms made way for new weaving machines, causing the resulting 1811–1816 UK uprisings by the so-called Luddites who feared for their livelihood because of technology.[71]

Historically, the benefits of automation often resulted in many new opportunities for those initially disturbed or replaced by it. Markets became more efficient, costs fell, industries and economies grew, new sectors were born, and over time, the industrial society did not really suffer sustained long-term technological unemployment because of new technologies or automation.[72] With each wave of industrialization, new technology enabled new sectors and eventually created enough new jobs to replace those old jobs which it had made redundant. Wages also increased along with productivity—at least until the Internet came along!

Fast forward to the information economy—now a truly ancient-sounding term used to describe the first wave of the Internet—and the relationship between technological gains and job creation took a different turn. Inequality increased in major economies—led by the US—as those that owned the means and platforms of digitization were able to make do with a lot less workers than ever before.[73] [74]

The transition from the information economy to the knowledge economy has been far shorter and potentially more disruptive. Now, as we take the next step and rush headlong into the machine intelligence economy, employment is expected to decline and the disparity between productivity and average wages is only likely to grow. By exploiting the Megashifts, businesses can make better products, much faster, at a lower cost. I predict that job-reducing disruptions and jobless growth may well become the norm, not the exception.

Some worrisome trends related to work have been noticeable since the early 1980s, when we saw the first waves of automation and machines that could do our work for us, starting with farming equipment, welding robots, and automated call centers. But the scale of the challenge is now becoming more apparent. The US Bureau of Labor Statistics reports that—since 2011—overall US productivity increased significantly but employment and wages did not.[75] As a result, corporate profits have risen since 2000.[76]

At the same time, inequality has exploded globally: According to *The Huffington Post,* the richest 62 people on the planet now have amassed more wealth than 50% of the world's entire population.[77]

The key question is whether continued exponential technological progress will exacerbate this worrisome trend, or whether it will somehow address it.

I think the US statistics may indicate a larger trend that is likely to be amplified dramatically by the Megashifts: Technological progress is no longer a catalyst of income and jobs as it was during the Industrial Age, and even during the early Information/Internet Age. Yes, margins and total profits rise for most companies as machines are increasingly substituting for people. However, those millions of laid-off workers don't seem to see any benefit from automation—truck drivers won't become mobile interface designers that easily!

Now imagine where this will take us based on exponential technological progress. A 2013 Oxford Martin School study suggests that up to 50% of jobs could be automated away in the next two decades.[78] Enterprise profits could then skyrocket because firms can decrease the number of people they employ globally, and this could be repeated across all industry sectors. In other words, by putting automation and the other nine Megashifts front and center, large business could potentially make a lot more money with a lot fewer people.

We will of course see some new jobs being created that did not previously exist, such as human-machine interface designers, cloud biologists, artificial intelligence (AI) supervisors, human genome analysts, and personal privacy managers. However, hundreds of millions of donkey-work roles and routine jobs, will be gone forever—particularly those that are mostly repetitive, and that do not require many human-only skills such as negotiation, creativity, or empathy. The question is not if but when.

This will become a definitive technology vs. humanity challenge: We need to realize how exponentially fast this change is likely to happen, and what it could mean for education, learning, training, government strategies, social benefit systems, and public policies around the globe.

As AIs gradually then suddenly become scientists, programmers, doctors, and journalists, meaningful work opportunities could become so scarce that very few of us would snag a job-as-we-know-it today. At the same time, most items on the lower steps of the Maslow's hierarchy of needs—such as food, water, and shelter—will become increasingly cheaper. Machines will be doing most of the hard work, making the provision of services such as transportation, banking, food, and media vastly cheaper. We may be heading towards the uncharted territory of economic abundance on the one hand, but the end of working for a living on the other. We will eventually need to separate money from occupation, and that shift will challenge some very central assumptions about how we define our own values and identities.

Will that be a good or a bad thing? How will people who cannot find work pay for the goods and services produced by the machines, even if they are much cheaper than today? Is this the end of consumption as the central logic behind capitalism? Are we seeing the beginning of the end of paid work as we knew it?

Politicians, public officials, and governments in general must become much more aware of the automation challenge, and must become much better stewards as we rush toward it. Thought leadership will be the most crucial requirement, and any public official who does not understand the need to become a "future steward" is losing the plot.

The chief reason whether we will vote for a political candidate in the very near future will be how well they manage the present, the "what is." while at the same time showing that they have a strong understanding of the "what might be."

## Automation$^2$–the five A's

I often think of automation as progressing in these five, progressively worsening steps:

1. Automation
2. Assentation
3. Abdication
4. Aggravation
5. Abomination

## Automation is an inevitable destination

I think that exponential automation is a certainty, simply because it is finally becoming possible, and it dramatically reduces costs—a primary focus in almost all businesses and organizations. We will see a new kind of low-cost, hyper-efficiency in most industries within the next five to ten years—think about what that could do to jobs and employment. But should efficiency really overrule humanity? Should we automate things just because we can? Should businesses that invest aggressively in replacing humans with technology pay some kind of automation tax that goes to benefit those that no longer have a job? These are questions we'll need to answer very soon.

Let's consider the fact that the combinatory forces of the Megashifts—especially digitization, virtualization, intelligization (deep learning and AI), and mobilization—are creating new possibilities for automation every single day. In early 2016, when Google's GoAlpha system cracked the gaming code, it was not programmed to play Go, but rather learned to play it from scratch, by itself.[79]

This is not narrow AI, pre-programmed computers that can beat humans in more-or-less mathematical or logical areas such as chess; this is AI that can use a more human-like neural network-based approach to mimic how the brain learns, and that can adapt and program itself. Imagine this kind of AI looking at very complex and large-scale human tasks and challenges, and then devising a way to solve and automate them for us—to be infinitely better than we are at pretty much any knowledge-related task.

In *Smarter than Us: the Rise of Machine Intelligence*, Stuart Armstrong writes:

> If an AI possessed any one of these skills—social abilities, technological development, economic ability—at a superhuman level, it is quite likely that it would quickly come to dominate our world in one way or another. And as we've seen, if it ever developed these abilities to the human level, then it would likely soon develop them to a superhuman level. So we can assume that if even one of these skills gets programmed into a computer, then our world will come to be dominated by AIs or AI-empowered humans.[80]

Take the example of social security, administering medical claims, pensions, and unemployment benefits for potentially hundreds of millions of people. Deploying AI, it may soon become feasible to have an intelligent supercomputer figure out what the rules of social security should be, and how they could be implemented, resulting in huge savings for governments but quite possibly dehumanizing citizens in the process.

In the US, an advanced AI could derive these rules by drawing on all the available social security data from the past 80-plus years since the social security system was founded in 1935.[81] It would also learn from all the other available data such as health records, social network profiles, legal backgrounds and regulations, along with city and government databases. A constantly evolving social security AI (call it SocSecBot) may be the result, one which can handle these very complex transactions, supported by maybe 10–20% of the current staff. Say goodbye to human empathy and compassion: Machines would be determining your pension benefits, and there would be very little arguing with them.

I often wonder what will happen when these concepts become reality, gradually then suddenly. Here is a likely chain of events that is already playing out in social media overload situations. After we encounter automation at every turn, we often start assentating, basically accepting the system's decisions and superiority—begrudgingly but with a smiling face. We are not really excited about it, but we won't make a big fuss.

Then, we may start abdicating, which means we "leave the throne" and give the power to the system. Pretty soon, we're not the most important entity in this system; the machine itself is becoming the new center of gravity—we have become the content rather than the reason. The tool has become the purpose, and we start doing things just to keep the system happy. Initially and primarily, "the system" will be the other nodes in the network, the humans that are also connected to the same global electronic ecosystem.

Facebook is currently the best example of abdication: Rather than taking any real political action, which would likely be quite cumbersome and often inconvenient, we simply "like" something on Facebook, share a video with our friends, sign a petition, or at best, donate a few dollars or euros to a Kickstarter or Causes.com campaign.

### Assentation

We already see many examples of the automation of things that should not be automated—such as using a software engine that crafts "better" messages in order for us to get more "likes" on social networks. We often experience assentation after the fact, after indiscriminately agreeing and going along for the ride by proxy because it's easy and convenient. It gets the job done. An example is adding a Facebook friend just because he's a friend of a friend of another friend and recently "liked" your post. Why not, and what's the damage? I'd agree, in this case, it would be hard to argue that there is any real damage.

## Abdication

Next, we may find ourselves, mostly inadvertently, abdicating responsibilities that used to be ours, and offloading or outsourcing them to technology. Rather than visiting your grandmother frequently, maybe you just set up Skype in her home and visit her that way, more often, but mediated via a screen. Is that a good or bad outcome?

Or, in the very near future, rather than making sure she visits the doctor regularly, you'll send her a remote diagnosis device that can measure her vitals anywhere, anytime, so that you do not have to take her to the doctor yourself, all the time.

Abdication (literally, "renouncing the throne") of our own power to hand over control to technology has become a constant theme all around us. I quite frequently use TripAdvisor, which tells me authoritatively that a particular restaurant is the best, and even though we are standing right in front of 25 other nice-looking places, we simply go where the machine tells us. In a way, we are transferring our authority and our own judgment to an algorithm. Again, in the case of TripAdvisor, not a big deal, but imagine this tendency growing exponentially, as well! It may end up feeling like things are no longer actually decided or even done by us—they just happen to us. It makes life so much easier, doesn't it? Going along takes a lot less effort than going alone.

I've had this particular TripAdvisor debate with many friends and audiences in the past couple of years, and I've come to the conclusion that if I use it as just another data point among many others, and if I am aware of the lures of assentation and abdication, then TripAdvisor is quite useful. Again, it's all about the balance. But what would I do if TripAdvisor became an AI, a smart bot-in-the-sky, and I could no longer actually judge its performance and honesty that easily? What if it became so smart that I would have no choice but to either trust it completely, or not at all?

Google Maps is another example of how easy it is to get humans to abdicate our thrones. Using Google Maps, how many times have you stood at an intersection in a strange city looking for something on the screen that was literally in front of you? But no, we don't believe our eyes and ears anymore—or other people's for that matter. We believe what the brain in the sky tells us. Will it rain, should I take an umbrella? The Google OS will tell me, rather than my own hunch about the weather, or a quick glance out of the window.

It is quite trivial in this case, yes, but consider the coming amplifications as a result of exponential technologies. Will we one day have a global medical brain deciding whether we should have children, based on our DNA and billions of other factors? Will insurance companies refuse coverage if we proceed anyway? Will we still be free to make decisions that are not based on logic and algorithms? Will we still be able to do stupid things such as drive too fast, drink too much, or eat the wrong food? Is free will dying?

### Now imagine Abdication²–forgetting ourselves exponentially

What would happen if technology continued to encourage us to give up even more control because it is so convenient, efficient, and magical? Not to mention 95% faster! What if we have seen only the tip of the iceberg on abdication, if we are at level five on a scale of 0–100? Might we eventually, as author Stephen Talbott suggests in *The New Atlantis,* "abdicate consciousness," allow machines to act as the ultimate arbitrator of values and morals?[82] If, as Talbott argues, "technologies powerfully invite us to forget ourselves," what will happen when we apply exponentially more powerful technologies?

Will this attraction towards "forgetting ourselves" become a default way of sleepwalking through digital life, opening the door to a kind of global digital feudalism—where the overlords of technology rule us in ways that are beyond our understanding?

One thing is certain: Technology and many of its biggest providers are doing whatever they can do to endear us to the paths of assentation and abdication, whether inadvertently or by design. We don't attempt to eat differently; instead, we take medication to help us deal with high blood pressure. We don't use boredom as an opportunity to contemplate; instead, we fill up the emptiness with our shiny new tablets, venturing out into the digital vortex. We don't look for opportunities to discover new friends for our children; instead, we let them make virtual friends using pet robots and Hello Barbie, the first doll that connects to a cloud-brain and talks to your kids like an actual person.[83] It's just so much easier!

Seen in this context, could intelligent digital assistants (IDA) such as Amazon Echo or Google Home soon prove to become abdication engines?

In the case of social security as discussed above, this abdication-compulsion might lead to government officials abdicating their responsibilities to the system. For example, let's suppose this imaginary SocSecBot gradually begins taking over human tasks because it is 90% cheaper and 1,000% faster. Even if it is only 90% correct, chances are that governments would say, "It's still so much better."

### Aggravation

The next step in this downward spiral might well be aggravation for both the few remaining human service agents and the system's users, customers, and clients. Frustration would rage but there would be little we could do about it because the system would be infinitely faster, more efficient, and scalable. Frustrations could be addressed, but given the overwhelming presence of the system in every part of our lives, there is almost zero chance we could actually stop using it.

Again, Facebook offers the best current example: While it is seriously aggravating to get a constant stream of irrelevant status updates by people that we barely remember, we still don't want to risk being disconnected from those that do matter to us. Once again, utter convenience and the sheer power and reach of the platform make it impossible for us to do anything about what is not working for us.

## Abomination

Finally, treating people in a social security environment just by the numbers, as disembodied data sources, is certain to eventually become an abomination, a perversion of the original intent of providing human (read: social) services to human citizens. This is the final, somewhat depressing stage of the five A's that we may reach if we don't address the first two stages (assentation and abdication) when we automate things.

One can only hope that technologically well-implemented and well-designed automation will result in lesser assentation and fewer abdications, with only the occasional aggravation. However, that is the scary thing about exponential automation—we won't even notice that we have lost our power and control before it has reached the pivot point, and by then we may have lost our own capabilities to do anything about it.

## Finding a balance

The issue is, yet again, finding the right balance: What can we automate that won't replace innate or indispensable human processes, conversations, or flows that we should not seek to abdicate? When contacting a call center to change your airline reservation, do you need the service agent to display human understanding or empathy? In most cases you don't, but in some cases you do, for example, if a courtesy issue arises. So call centers may well end up 90% automated in the next few years, but in some cases we will still need actual human interactions. In this particular case, well-designed and human-supervised automation is probably a positive evolution but millions of jobs will be lost, no matter how you look at it.

Taking this debate just a few steps further and only slightly into the future ... when traveling on an airplane, would you trust a fully automated, pilotless cockpit? Would you feel safer if a human pilot were still present? When being diagnosed for a medical problem, do you need "humanness" and compassion, or would you be okay with a machine telling you just the facts? In cases like flu or a stomach problem, it seems that automation-enabling remote diagnosis could be useful and socially acceptable. However, when diagnosing complex challenges such as stress symptoms, asthma, or diabetes, such automation would certainly tend to dehumanize medical care.

It won't simply be about saying yes or no to automation; it will be about gradual responses and an overall precautionary approach, striking a balance and putting human concerns first, always. The key question isn't whether or how technology can automate something, but how the outcome would feel for us humans, and whether automation would support human flourishing or not. It's about whether we are rooting for Team Human or Team Technology.

### Inviting automation inside?

Alongside all the things that are automating around us, there are a good many that are likely to automate within us, impacting how we think and what we feel. Consider how algorithms and software, IDAs, and AI-powered cloud services or robots are increasingly taking over our everyday affairs, and how some of us have already automated friendship via social networks or messaging apps.

For example, what will happen to our collective intelligence—the human dialogues through which we currently educate, debate, discuss, decide, and design our societies and democracies? How will our choices be shaped if what we see and hear about each other is determined purely by algorithms that are designed to make you stay and view ads as long as possible, rather than by people? What if these tools are not publicly controlled, supervised or regulated...?

Will we be influenced by machines and algorithms owned by a handful of giant global Internet platforms and technology companies? Will they become "virtual dopamine dispensing systems," programmed for stickiness and positive affirmation, and designed to achieve maximum results for their owners, advertisers, and other "data-miners" who want to analyze and exploit our personal data?

To wit, Google News[84] is not curated primarily by people, and neither is Facebook's so-called newsfeed[85] nor Baidu's news app.[86] In almost all cases, some human supervision is involved, but the algorithms do most of the actual work. At these companies, very few people are actually dealing with content in the traditional journalistic sense—instead they focus on devising ever-smarter algorithms and software to deal with each new requirement. No wonder Marc Andreessen's tagline, "software is eating the world," has already mutated to "Facebook is eating the Internet."[87] And Facebook does not plan to do the eating with people! Apart from programmers, engineers, and AI researchers, it wants to hire as few people as possible to deal with actual human customers.

Maybe sometime very soon, software will no longer just "eat the world" but increasingly "cheat the world." I already feel a bit cheated, or shall we say manipulated, when looking at my Facebook newsfeed, because I cannot trust it like I would trust *The New York Times, The Economist, Der Spiegel,* or *The Guardian*—its only purpose is to create benefit for itself. It isn't mass media, it's cheat media—and even though we are aware of it, we seem to be stuck with it.

It is not entirely one-way traffic—Mashable reports that Apple is putting considerable effort into using some human curation for its news app, music recommendation, and playlist services, but this is certainly an exception, not the rule.[88]

Automation is exploding because it's abundantly clear that humans are expensive, slow, and often inefficient, whereas machines are cheap, fast, ultra-efficient, and becoming exponentially more so. We cannot overestimate where this will take us in the next ten years. While productivity will explode, it seems inevitable that human employment as we know it will decline dramatically. We are certain to have occupations in the future, but they are likely to be disconnected from making a living.

It is also becoming quite likely that, on such fully automated news and media platforms, we will no longer see things that another, possibly more knowledgeable person thought we should see. Instead, content will be selected by a bot, an AI approximating what we should see, based on hundreds of millions of facts and data crumbs, analyzed in real time. The clear risk is that such services will be increasingly devoid of human notions of values, morals, ethics, emotions, art, or indeed the somewhat ephemeral principles of human storytelling.

Sure, bots and AIs will also be able to understand our emotions and feelings in the very near future, and they will eventually be able to simulate such emotions and storytelling abilities as well—but I believe they will still not achieve a state of being human.

I am not harking back to a golden age of the printed newspaper—they were and are impractical and often monopolistic, corrupt, or misleading. However, in many cases, the writers and editors were people whose job it was to know better than us, journalists who could see the broader context and could determine its relevance. Their mission was to focus solely on what the audience should see, as subjective as that may have been.

Clearly the Iraq weapons of mass destruction fiasco—presented by the likes of *Fox News* and many others—showed that channels and human correspondents could also be misleading and not without an agenda. However, at least we had a chance of understanding what and who it was behind a story, and a chance to question them. I believe no such possibility exits with AI newsbots. This much I'm certain of: We wouldn't even have a clue how to question them.

Another consequence of automated newsfeeds is that we will no longer see, or hear, the same content that people around us see—our families, spouses, friends, and colleagues. Their feeds will be 100% customized and possibly completely different from ours. Indeed, we are finally reaching the point where we have enough computing power to customize everyone's feed according to their fully personalized data.

Are we now boosting the often-decried "Internet filter bubble" problem, creating echo chambers of like-minded people whom algorithms have gathered together for us, so that we have the most pleasurable experience possible? What will that do for confirmation bias? Do the providers of such gigantic content algorithms—like Google and Facebook—consider such issues? Or are human concerns about filtering, manipulation, and biases the very last thing on these news providers' priority list?

"Well . . . ethics are nice to have; but we just don't have the time or resources for it right now," is what I hear from many companies when we discuss this. I believe this is a huge mistake because I fear a society with infinite technological power and no ethics is doomed.

Let's imagine this kind of NewsBot or MediaAI moving from online news to television, which is certain to happen. Picture the possible scenario: news programs customized for every single one of us via over-the-top (OTT) transmission using the Internet rather than terrestrial broadcasting or cable; *CNN* or public TV news in Europe replacing your Twitter video stream or Facebook video feed; apps, bots, and IDAs killing cable and traditional broadcasting as we know it. In less than ten years, TV and the Internet will have converged completely, making it entirely possible to completely tilt the way we consume media—and yes, there are many positives about the global trend towards OTT media as well, so let's not throw out the baby with the bath water!

If, as *Wired* founding executive editor and maverick Kevin Kelly once said, "machines are for answers and humans are for questions,"[89] then where will machines take us when it's about media, content, and information? Will they simply build a beautifully fake or simulated landscape of answers, filtering out all the questions we should and would have asked if there had been any wiggle room or empty space for contemplation?

> *"Computers are useless. They can only give you answers."*
> *–Pablo Picasso*[90]

In my view, we are distinguished by distinctly human traits such as the ability to ask questions, to imagine that something could be different, to be critical, to look at things from different angles, to read between the lines, and to see what may not yet be there. And aren't these what amazing content and media, and the people behind them, are meant to do?

I fear the moment when all these traits get lost because machines on every platform are programming what and whom we individually see, at all times. Then, we may be well on the way towards abdicating consciousness altogether and outsourcing our humanness. And we may be living in a kind of programmed reality before we know it—run by those who own the programs and servers.

*"Humans are the reproductive organs of technology."*
*–Kevin Kelly,* What Technology Wants[91]

If bots and AI do most of our thinking and increasingly act on our behalf, what would happen to the very process of how we make decisions? If many seemingly trivial decisions such as what movie I watch tonight, or what food I buy, are effectively made by software and intelligent agents, what would happen to surprises, mystery, mistakes, and serendipity? Could those IDAs be programmed to be human in the sense of random, individual, flawed, biased . . . and still generate results? And would we want them to achieve that?

Would bots end up voting on our behalf, and represent us in important democratic functions such as in referendums or even in parliaments? Would our IDAs gather the evidence and then use it to advise us on which way we should vote—based on our past views, behavior, and choices?

Will free will be a thing of the past because anything and everything can be predicted?

*"You realize, there is no free will in anything we create*
*with Artificial Intelligence . . ." –Clyde DeSouza[92]*

### Will wormholes rule the world?

As technology offers the potential to dive deeper into its wormhole, I see a significant danger in what exponential automation might be teaching us: We can shortcut almost everything by applying large datasets, AI, and robotics to it. No need for all that laborious, slow, and tedious "human stuff."

First, in my hands, then on my face, upon my ears, and finally inside my head. No need for kids to learn how to write because computers will just listen to, record, and transcribe everything we say to them. No need to deal with the complexities of real-life human relationships if I can have relationships and even sex with their digital equivalents using augmented reality, virtual reality, and robots. No need to learn how to play an instrument because my brain-computer interface (BCI) will allow me to make music just by thinking about it. No need to learn languages because my translation app is always ready to help. No need to talk to people if I can just get a data dump from them. No need for emotions that keep throwing a monkey wrench into the AI's good work.

Using automation, we can now reduce all the work it took to do many routinely human things, and get the same results instantaneously—at least that's the thinking. We can scan thousands of Twitter feeds and watch the best snippets from hundreds of YouTube videos on any given topic, and seemingly be an expert in no time. We can learn anything and everything "just in time" rather than "just in case." We just need the right input and the right program.

We flow with data rather than download and memorize knowledge. In a way, we can become superhuman. Or not?

I call these kinds of concepts wormholing because like a wormhole in the cosmos—an imaginary shortcut through space and time (entered via warp drive for all you *Star Trek* fans)—they represent the notion of bypassing all that tedious human stuff and getting to the goal much quicker by using technology.

But remember: It won't be human to do too much wormholing— or any at all, for that matter—because it will require us to become machines ourselves—at least partially. The Nobel prize-winning psychologist Daniel Kahneman points out repeatedly that "cognition is embodied—we think with the body, not the brain."[93] We must realize and accept that humanness is a holistic experience; that learning is interdependent on many factors, not just data feeds; that really powerful realizations happen in conversations, not usually in a stream of mouse clicks, although those can of course be useful, as well. In other words, if we remove the process from the result, we won't be getting the same results—we will have been cheated by software.

*"Human relationships are rich and they're messy and they're demanding. And we clean them up with technology. Texting, email, posting, all of these things let us present the self as we want to be. We get to edit, and that means we get to delete, and that means we get to retouch the face, the voice, the flesh, the body—not too little, not too much, just right." –Sherry Turkle*[94]

If we remove all the work required and all those tedious human behaviors like discussion, pondering, and emotions, what would that do to our collective humanness? Would we become completely dependent on those wormholes and warp drives, regardless of the fact that all they could ever really do is simulate a human experience?

Because the Megashifts (see chapter 3) work together in exponential and combinatorial ways, there is a huge challenge in front of us: Increasing digitization, automation, and virtualization will drive even more automation. That's because once a single step of the process is automated, it will force all other pieces to do the same. Automation of one step actuates the next, and the automation of an entire process triggers a chain reaction amongst those that it connects to. The logic cannot be broken because the system would try to route around it.

The end result could be that when we automate news and information, when we automate purchases and commerce, when we automate financial decisions and medical care, we will eventually need to be automated ourselves—so that we don't disrupt the system too much.

Whether it's our computer, our smartphone, our IDA, or our AI, if we allow the tools to become our purpose, causing us to abdicate and delegate all authority to them, then we will be well on the path to being dispensable because, as humans, we will make lousy machines.

*"The strongest argument for why advanced AI needs a body may come from its learning and development phase—scientists may discover it's not possible to 'grow' AGI without some kind of body." –James Barrat,* Our Final Invention: Artificial Intelligence and the

End of the Human Era[95]

So how do we draw the boundaries of automation and what might be considered a step too far into the wormhole? To get the conversation started, here are some examples of what I believe should and could be automated:

- Bookkeeping, filing, and financial administration
- Airport security
- Diary management—scheduling appointments and meetings
- Other routine tasks that don't involve human decision making

Activities that I think should not be automated (assuming that we could) may include:

- Public news and media
- Messages to one's personal connections
- Likes and affirmations on social media
- Friendship (as in Twitter auto-follow)
- Hiring or firing people
- Partner selection and forming of relationships
- Democracy (as in signing online petitions in lieu of political activities)
- Human genome alteration
- Giving birth

As a reminder, the textbook definition of "to automate" is to literally "act of oneself, to act unadvisedly."[96] Clearly, there are numerous tasks, actions, and activities where automation brings value and benefit to all. Then there are those automations that bring benefit to many, those that benefit a tiny few, and finally those that disadvantage practically everyone in the long run. In *The Time Machine*, H.G. Wells imagined a future starkly divided between feral Morlocks and ineffectual but elite Eloi.[97] Even if we all escape the way of the Morlock, how sovereign or heroic will we feel as Eloi—as passive meatware with titular mastery?

# Chapter 5
# The Internet of Inhuman Things

*Will the Internet of Inhuman Things gradually and then suddenly require us to forgo our humanity and become ever more mechanistic just to remain relevant?*

As discussed previously, a combination of technological developments is fueling the emergence of the Internet of Things (IoT)—also described by Cisco as the Internet of Everything and by others like GE as the Industrial Internet.

The promise is simple: When everything is connected and data is being collected everywhere, all the time, we will be able to discover new truths and even predict and prevent events. Privacy and security expert Bruce Schneier calls this artificial brain-in-the-cloud of interconnected devices, sensors, hardware, and processes the "World-Sized Web."[98] Indeed, it may well deliver a new era of optimization and hyper-efficiency, but what will happen to human interactions?

The IoT promises enormous cost savings through a future of greater sustainability in a circular economy where all resources are reused, repaired, or recycled after initial consumption, and waste is effectively eliminated.[99] The IoT is enabled by embedding sensors in every object and connecting virtually everyone and everything. Then, by deploying artificial intelligence (AI) and predictive analytics, the idea is to achieve a meta-intelligence through an exponentially better ability to read, understand, and apply data.

My conversations with IoT proponents around the world suggest that, if it delivers on its promise, we could realize savings of 30–50% on global logistics and shipping costs; 30–70% of the costs of personal mobility and transportation; 40–50% of energy, heating, and air-conditioning expenses—and that's just for starters.

The potential economic benefits of this connectivity are tantalizing: The IoT is truly a gigantic undertaking and will certainly dwarf the previous "Internet of humans + computers."

*Nothing vast enters the life of mortals without a curse.*
*–Sophocles[100]*

The IoT is bound to be orders of magnitude more powerful than the human Internet of today, and therefore infinitely more likely to cause unintended consequences. The outcome of global deployment of the IoT could be heaven or hell, but either way the compass for this journey is being calibrated right now.

### Could the IoT turn us into things?
We already have many negative side effects of the Internet to deal with today. Let's assume the unintended consequences of surveillance, loss of privacy, and "digital obesity" were indeed not intentional. Faced with the global uptake of the IoT, one must certainly start to wonder how much more power (access to our data and the AI to process it) we want to give to the providers of these solutions, tools, engines, and platforms. We must also ask how these protections can be accomplished without global agreements, effective sanctions, self-regulation, and independent supervision.

The leading US-based platforms, cloud service providers, and other technology companies already seem incapable of preventing the NSA, FBI, and other officials from scanning all our devices and data. So how might this play out in five to seven years when we could have over 200 billion connected devices?

In its darkest variation, the IoT could be the climax of machine thinking—the most perfect spying operating system (OS) ever devised, the largest real-time surveillance network ever contrived, enforcing total human compliance and killing off all remaining semblance of anonymity.[101]

Just imagine a world, not too far off, where:

- Your connected car communicates all of its data in real time, including its location and all your movements in the cockpit;
- All your payments are linked to your smart devices, with cash, wallets, and credit cards a thing of the past;
- Your doctor can easily find out how little you have gotten off your chair and walked this week, and what your heart rate was while you slept on the plane;
- Your external brains (aka mobile devices) are now directly connected to your wetware brain via wearables, brain-computer interfaces (BCI), or implants;
- Everyone and everything becomes a data beacon, generating thousands of gigabytes per day, collected, filtered, and analyzed in the cloud by armies of IBM's Watsons and Google's DeepMinds applying their hungry, self-learning global AI brains every second.

Efficiency would likely trump humanity at every turn, and we would eventually be governed by a giant machine OS that self-learns and literally feeds off our output until even that contribution is no longer needed; at which point we would become worth less than the technology that we created and fed.

The innate sovereignty that has defined mankind for at least tens of thousands of years will finally be compromised—not by any external creature or by alien visitors, but by technology protagonists and their hyper-mechanization agendas.

If we, today, cannot even agree on what the rules and ethics should be for an Internet of people and their computing devices, how would we agree on something that is potentially a thousand times as vast?

Should we not be more worried about proceeding just because we can?

## Who is in control?

Today we have standards, guidelines, agreements, and treaties on what is permitted in biotechnology and bioengineering—such as the 1975 Asilomar guidelines on recombinant DNA.[102] We also have nuclear nonproliferation treaties. We don't yet have any such thing for data and intelligence—the oil of the Digital Age. Despite the fact that data is quickly becoming the single most powerful economic driver, we do not yet have a global treaty on what is allowed with the personal data of the Internet's 3.4 billion users,[103] or a treaty on cognitive computing or artificial general intelligence. With the exception of nuclear weapons, rarely in the course of human history has so much been ventured at such speed with so little reflection. Indeed, the exponential use of data, and now AI, will soon rival the impact of nuclear weapons, yet AI remains a largely unregulated space.

Who will make sure that the leading data and AI companies are doing the right thing? Who will make sure that the entities running the shiny new IoT are doing the right thing? And what is the right thing; who defines it? Will we even be able to distinguish the right from the wrong thing?

## Androrithms and the precautionary principle

What will keep the new masters of the universe from turning not just processes and hardware into data, but also turning humans into things, either by accident or by design? The technology industry's delight with the IoT and its obvious benefits notwithstanding, this is a risk we should not take without exercising extreme caution and consideration.

We need to insert balances that ensure a truly human development process, tempering every exponential progress step of technology with human concerns, throwing a human monkey wrench between the 0s and 1s that are starting to dominate our lives.

I humbly suggest we apply an updated version of the precautionary principle (see chapter 8) to those who aim to power and provide the blessings of the IoT: The burden to prove and ensure that the IoT will not harm those subjected to it should be placed on those in control, and only once that responsibility is secured should we move ahead. At the same time, we should allow for proactionary approaches as well, and not stifle innovation.

This is no longer a question of either/or—nor is it a question of simply blending these strategies. *Homo sapiens* are now in altogether unknown territory, 70 years after unleashing nuclear power upon the Earth in a still controversial military experiment and political decision. Without any new world war to justify or excuse our headlong advance into "big dataland," we are proceeding as if all the choices will remain available to us. The Internet of Inhuman Things could surround our humanity and alter its essential essence—just as it will impart godlike omnipotence to its owners. We need to take precautions, and we need to remain proactive—but these can no longer be two separate agendas, driven by two separate tribes.

# Chapter 6
# Magic to Manic to Toxic

*As we rave through the all-night honeymoon party that is tech, it's salutary to think about the price to be paid tomorrow, and forever.*

Back in 1961, one of the godfathers of futurism and a great influence on my own work, Arthur C. Clarke, famously said, "Any sufficiently advanced technology is indistinguishable from magic."[104] Today, as highlighted in the previous chapters, we are beginning to see what Clarke envisaged with this prescient statement: We are in the midst of a veritable magic explosion; science and technology are delivering advances beyond our wildest imagination.

The magical effects of technology have become a big deal, commercially, economically, and socially, powering the meteoric rise and stock market success of companies such as Google, Apple, Facebook, Amazon, Baidu, Tencent, and Alibaba. Technological magic is also the driver and key enabler of predominantly US and Chinese unicorns and decacorns—disruptive companies such as Baidu, Dropbox, Uber, and Airbnb that are relatively recent arrivals on the scene.

When Google first launched in 1998, finding the perfect result to a search query on "cheap flights to London" was considered a kind of magic. So was being able to order almost any book, anywhere in the world, and have it arrive at your doorstep within a few days. The next wave of innovation saw the emergence of magical, legal, and very low-cost entertainment platforms such as Netflix, Hulu, ViaPlay,

Spotify, and YouTube, changing the way we consume media—and if or what we pay for it—forever.

Magic moments are everywhere now. Just activate the Shazam app and hold up your smartphone to any source of music. Shazam will identify what song is playing, and will then connect you to any digital music platform you might be using in order to save the song for later listening or sharing. This simple challenge of identifying or discovering new music used to be infinitely more complicated; now it's easier than making a phone call.

For most of us, mobile devices and apps are, of course, the number one manifestation of technological magic: It often seems that "there is (or must be) an app for that" has become a kind of default response to pretty much any challenge we face in our daily lives—as long as we are connected to broadband mobile Internet, with a powerful mobile device (which is pretty much always).

On the Apple app store alone, you can use tens of thousands of apps to edit your images and hundreds just for dating. There are countless apps for scheduling and appointments, apps that help you get divorced, several very useful wet-diaper notification services (like Tweetpee), numerous applications allowing you to practice digital voodoo remotely, and—most important—all kinds of fart simulators!

Around the globe, magic is what powers technology, what drives the mobile device business, and why a smartphone is now more important than a computer. The pyramid of Maslow's hierarchy of needs has changed accordingly: Alongside basic needs such as food, drink, clothing, and shelter, we must now include mobile devices, smartphones, and Wi-Fi connectivity—often ranking even higher than sex, friendship, and prestige! In the not too distant future, it seems inevitable that we will add intelligent digital assistants (IDA) to that hierarchy, as well.

With the advent of the Internet of Things (IoT), autonomous vehicles (self-driving cars), artificial intelligence (AI) and intelligent assistants, even everyday things and processes will acquire magical powers. For example, Libelium, a leading B2B magic provider, seeks to bring the world to life by enabling smart farming, smart cities, and smart energy.[105] It does this by setting up vast sensor networks and making pretty much any previously "dumb" device or piece of hardware intelligent, whether it's a tractor on the field or a tree in the park.

With smart solutions, every pipeline knows how hot it is, how much gas is flowing through it, how noisy it is outside, and much more. Every streetlight knows how many cars and people pass by it, what Bluetooth MAC addresses keep showing up, or what the level of pollution is—you name it, you equip it, and the smart environment can identify and measure it. Given the potential payoff, it's little wonder that every technology company is putting major investment behind the IoT.

Magic is set to drive a scale and speed of technology adoption beyond even our most extreme expectations. The iPhone is (was?) magic—indeed, for a good many people it was once the definition of magic. The iPad is magic, augmented reality (AR) and virtual reality (VR) are magic (2016 marks the gradual then sudden rise of both), Tesla cars are magic, Microsoft's HoloLens is magic . . . new kinds of magic are popping up every other minute.

Crucially, the cost of all this magic is falling—this is very important as, a bit like illegal drugs, the price and wide availability of a magical offering always has material impact on how fast and deep it spreads. In five years, magic that used to be hugely expensive, such as human genome analysis or maybe even some form of supercomputing, will be dirt cheap. Just imagine what that will do to the way we live: a personal magic kingdom available to each of us. Every problem solved by technology. Becoming as God.

### Magical humans—intelligence inside

Now, technological magic is starting to transcend the realm of hardware and stuff—it's no longer only about devices, gadgets, services, or connectivity. Increasingly it's about us, our bodies, our minds, our humanity.

A large number of researchers have recently presented evidence on how the Internet, and in particular the magic of social networks, actually causes us to have very real physical reactions.[106] They have found that endorphins and dopamine rush through our bodies because some stranger thousands of miles away has "liked" our post or posted a comment that made us feel worthy and appreciated. Apparently, this is very much a preset biological reaction that occurs without effort and may not be subject to conscious control, and it seems to be one of the reasons that a number of the social networks are becoming more valuable than many retailers or e-commerce sites.

Facilitating this kind of pleasure trap is a key intent when mixing the secret sauce of the leading social networks.[107] And it's one of the chief reasons why, in January 2016, I considered seriously dialing back on Facebook, myself—being emotionally and intellectually manipulated by their algorithms seemed like a very comfortable road towards a bizarre kind of inhumanity. Albeit, after six weeks I realized I could not afford to ignore the fact that Facebook drives 60% of the traffic to my websites so this is indeed a challenging problem that needs further observation. For now, I continue to post things but have pretty much stopped using Facebook as a source of news or as a medium.

Apart from the obvious role of magic in social networking, magic-by-technology is increasingly the universal driver of fast adoption because it gets our juices flowing and cranks up our senses. As we review the videos that our GoPro cameras have shot from the wild mountain-bike trip in Arizona, we feel the magic tingling. The magic of WhatsApp allows us to connect instantly to our loved ones for free—anywhere on the globe—and share all those other magical moments with them.

### So what is the big deal?

Sure, many of these technologies are generally to be welcomed, and of course I enjoy many of them quite frequently myself. Technology addiction, overuse, and social awkwardness have been a concern in the past few years, but mostly as a fairly benign issue, or something that is often attributed to various Luddite-types, offliners, and digital detox promoters. I'm often asked what the big deal is, and why too much technological magic is an issue, so please allow me to share a few thoughts.

### Exponential tech will soon trigger a chain of "A-bomb challenges"

I believe that today we are positioned right at the inflection point of this exponential curve of technological development, and it represents a pivotal time in history. In some respects, our scientists and technologists are in a similar situation to that faced by Albert Einstein. While he considered himself a pacifist, in 1939–1940 he still urged President Roosevelt to speed up building the nuclear bomb before the Germans would. In 1941, Einstein inadvertently contributed to the development of the nuclear bomb by helping Vannevar Bush solve some intricate mathematical problems that were slowing down the US atomic program.[108]

The historian Doug Long comments:

> Einstein biographer Ronald Clark has observed that the atomic bomb would have been invented without Einstein's letters, but that without the early US work that resulted from the letters, the A-bombs might not have been ready in time to use during the war on Japan.[109]

In November 1954, five months before his death, Einstein summarized his feelings about his role in the creation of the atomic bomb:

> I made one great mistake in my life . . . when I signed the letter to President Roosevelt recommending that atom bombs be made; but there was some justification—the danger that the Germans would make them.[110]

*"The human spirit must prevail over technology."*
*–Albert Einstein[111]*

Analogous arguments to "Einstein 1939" are being presented to justify the accelerated pursuit of ultra-high-stakes exponential technologies such as artificial general intelligence, geo-engineering (controlling the weather by means of technology), the deployment of autonomous weapon systems, and human genetic modification. The most common arguments I keep hearing are that, "If we don't do this, someone else (and probably someone evil) surely will, and we will be left behind," and, "Apart from all these dangers, these technologies will do a world of good—it would be foolish not to harness them," and, "There is no way to un-invent something or simply stop inventing. Attempting to create it, if indeed it can be invented—that's just human nature."

My reply is always the same: Technology is neither good nor bad; it simply is. We must—now and here—decide and agree which exact use is evil or not.

As you read this, technologies even more powerful than nuclear energy or atomic weapons are being invented and tested in multiple domains. Rapid advances seem inevitable and will not be stopped by merely pointing to the need to apply the precautionary principle of holding those inventing a new technology responsible to prove its harmlessness first (see chapter 8).

I believe the key challenge is this: How do we make sure these inevitable technological accomplishments remain 98% magical, i.e. that they will be used for the benefit of collective human flourishing and not suddenly flip to the evil side? Think of breakthroughs like gene editing that might prevent the development of cancer. Now imagine the potential use of the very same advances to create human-animal chimeras, leading to the dramatic rise of cyborgs (man-machine beings) or allowing us to self-determine our genetic make-up.

These endeavors could be very much like the use of nuclear power to develop atomic bombs, with multiple "digital Hiroshimas" becoming a distinct possibility.

What will be the ethical guidelines? Do we even agree on some kind of ethical foundation, globally? How will we get all nations to agree on defining or constraining the dark sides of technological development? Who will be in charge of monitoring violations, and in general, how could we prevent a deadly spiral towards what author James Barrat calls "our final inventions"?[112] This is why the debate on digital ethics is essential (see chapter 10).

Exponential growth in data, information, connectivity, and intelligence are the new oil of the digital world, powering dramatic shifts in every aspect of our world. As such, we are now crossing the threshold from mere mathematical calculations or computer code to nuclear strike-like capabilities.

> *"One cubic inch of nanotube circuitry, once fully developed,*
> *would be up to one hundred million times more powerful*
> *than the human brain." –Ray Kurzweil,* The Singularity
> is Near: When Humans Transcend Biology[113]

Science and technology have already equipped us with immense power. In the next 20–30 years we will see a series of pivot points on the exponential curve, such as ubiquitous quantum computing and the advent of the so-called Singularity. As we progress up the curve at an accelerating pace, we will become infinitely more powerful, giving us capabilities beyond our wildest imaginations. Paraphrasing what many are reported to have said through history, from Voltaire to Superman's father: "With great power comes great responsibility."[114]

First and foremost, how can the tremendous power of exponential technologies be harnessed to advance human happiness? How can we ensure that an equal amount of effort is spent on understandings, agreements, and rules that will protect us from manic or toxic results? How should we define where the magic ends?

### Welcome to the magic explosion

Once what I like to call the magic quotient is upped exponentially, these until-now latent problems regarding the abuse or evil use of a given technology will become magnified—perhaps exponentially—again, gradually then suddenly.

While I am still optimistic about our collective abilities to channel the power of exponential technologies, I am also concerned that, in almost every instance of exponential and combinatorial change, there is a real risk that we may go from magic to manic to toxic in a very short timeframe.

Thus, we simply cannot afford bad stewardship during these times. The challenge to our humanity is looming larger every day, the magic quotient is exploding, and the manic is never far away.

### The key question is no longer if or how, but why?

As discussed, we are now at the pivot point of exponential and combinatorial progress where total human well-being could either be magnified or greatly diminished by technology. Soon the question will no longer be if or how some technological magic can actually be realized—the answer will almost always be yes. The key emerging questions are why should it be done, who will be in charge or control it, and what it may mean for the future of humanity?

To maintain an environment that actually furthers human flourishing, we must give deep consideration to unintended consequences and the default inclusion of externalities. We must start paying attention to those side effects and externalities that are usually and often understandably not initially part of the business model per se, such as assessing impacts on global warming as a consequence of our dependence on fossil fuel. We must accelerate the rise of these issues up the corporate agenda, and holistic thinking must become our default approach.

A magic explosion is just about to happen as technology becomes super-powerful and super-fast beyond imagination, rendering us godlike. Intelligent digital assistants will soon become super-intelligent, omnipresent, dirt cheap, invisible, and embedded into absolutely everything—including ourselves.

Where we are today differs in a critical way from past phases of technology-enabled magic. In particular, exponential and combinatorial developments will deliver magic that differs in sheer size, scope, and kind from anything we have ever witnessed or could conceive of. Using a search engine to find a great deal for a hotel room is one thing, but it's quite a different cup of tea to have the entire travel booking process done for you by the IDA successors to the tools we use today such as Apple's Siri, Microsoft's Cortana, Facebook's M, or IPSoft's Amelia. The current wave of IDAs will seem like the first Ford Model Ts when compared to today's Ferraris and Teslas. You ain't seen nothing yet!

### Technology goes internal–separating us from the world, increasingly disconnecting us from human experiences

The traditional search engine is about using an external tool, like using a hammer to build a house, while the IDA approach is about letting the hammer design the house itself. The technology is becoming akin to our own brain, moving itself inside of us. The distinction between the tool and us is vanishing.

You may already have observed the trend towards using IDAs to do the work for us. Siri can answer our questions and instantly direct us to resources, Alexa can order books for us and read them aloud, Amelia can book our travel for us. Intelligent digital assistants are the next apps, and they will become widespread in the next few years.

Now just imagine what degree of separation, personal disconnection, deskilling, and general abdication we might encounter with our free, omnipresent, and hyper-intelligent assistants:

- They will know who we are—and I mean truly know every data point, every communication, every movement, every digital breadcrumb;
- They will know literally everything about our areas of interest, intentions, and desires at this very moment, whether they are about a mere transaction, a meeting, or anything else;
- They will be able to speak to millions of other assistants to create an extremely powerful network effect—a global-brain-in-the-sky;
- They will be able to communicate in 50-plus languages on our behalf. And that's just for starters.

*"Digiphrenia—the way our media and technologies encourage us to be in more than one place at the same time." –Douglas Rushkoff,* Present Shock: When Everything Happens Now[115]

There is no doubt that the sheer speed, power, fun, and convenience of these IDAs will be utterly irresistible—and I think it will almost certainly lead to human deskilling and emotional detachment on a gigantic scale. IDAs will pick up from where smartphones end, bringing the computing interface into the private realm of our thoughts, our anticipation, and our habitual behavior. From there, it's just a short hop to direct-brain interfaces and hybrid humanity.

Consider 3D printing, for instance: If we could print a fantastic meal instantly, would we still do the cooking? If we had an instant translation device, would we still learn languages? If we could command a computer with our brainwaves, would we still learn how to type? If necessity is the mother of invention, is choice the father of abdication?

Having the power of a 1970s mainframe computer the size of a living room in the palm of your hand, as we do with iPhones and Android devices today, is already mindboggling. Just imagine the quantum power of one million such devices available in the smart cloud, spontaneously through voice, gesture, or even thought command via a brain–computer interface (BCI).

As this magic explosion happens:

- Almost everything will be perceived or defined as a service because everything is digitized, automated, and intelligized. This will have huge economic impact as it progressively creates abundance in almost every sector of society—first music, movies, and books, followed by transportation, money, and financial services, and eventually, medical treatments, food, and energy. I believe that abundance will eventually cause the collapse of capitalism as we know it, and ring in a yet to be defined era of post-capitalism.

- We humans will become extremely powerful—and extremely dependent on those tools, so much so that, just like air or water, we will not function without them.
- We will constantly be tempted to reduce or completely abolish human idiosyncrasies such as contemplation or imagination because they appear to slow us down (and everyone else, as well).
- We will become sitting ducks for manipulation and undue influence by anyone who knows how to use the system.
- We will be well on our way to becoming machines so that we can still fit into the mechanized world.
- As biology gives way to technology, our biological systems will become increasingly optional, replaceable, and finally even vestigial.
- With technology becoming the world's dominant platform— easily and ubiquitously providing the "one truth according to tech"—our own cultures, inherited symbols, behaviors, and rituals could lapse into disuse.

Clearly, the question is whether such exponential technologies would actually still be tools. I argue they would not, for in the case of a hammer, or even in the case of electricity or the Internet itself, we would indeed be inconvenienced if the tool was no longer available— but we would not be fundamentally incapable of living. Electricity and Internet access are simply not as important as oxygen or water; they just make our lives a lot better.

Just like oxygen, though, many exponential technologies will no longer be considered tools; rather, they may soon be seen as vital requirements, at which point we may cease to be naturally or fully human. And this is where I think we need to draw the line. This is where we are on our way to becoming technology ourselves because these technologies will be as vital to us as breathing. I believe this is a line we should not cross—at least not involuntarily or by mere chance. While it might be reasonable for someone to become part machine because of an accident or a disease, doing so voluntarily or by design would be an entirely different thing.

Just imagine life following such a magic explosion—new tools a million times more powerful than we have today, for next-to-free, anytime, anywhere. Unfathomable. Irresistible. Addictive. Should we just yield to such a development and—as many technologists suggest—embrace the inevitable and complete convergence of man and machine, or should we take a more proactive role and really shape what we do or don't create?

Are we destined to become technology ourselves because the magic is finally going to enter our bodies? Let's ask some simple questions: Who would want to be without such magic, ever? Would we feel handicapped or inferior if our magical technologies were absent or unavailable? Would we then feel as limited as if we had suddenly lost our hearing or eyesight? Would we naturally accept these technologies as extensions of ourselves just as we've already done with smart mobile devices? Would our understanding of what is us and non-us (i.e. Them or It) fade completely? What would this total mediazation mean for our experience of the world around us? For our decision making? For our emotional world?

How will we respond?

I am concerned that we are already starting to confuse the magic of the tools with the drug-like effect of constant connectivity, mediazation, screenification, simulation, and virtualization. The magic is already becoming manic—addictive, tempting, nudging, demanding—so what will happen when the magic quotient reaches 1,000, when technology becomes infinitely more powerful, cheap, and inseparable from us?

> *"First we build the tools, then the tools build us." –Marshall McLuhan*[116]

I fear we are entering a period of exponential development that, if unrestrained, cannot possibly end in human happiness as defined by Aristotle's deeper, eudaemonian sense of human connection and contribution (see chapter 9). I fear this would be a reduction, not an expansion, of who we are: no longer an empowerment but an enslavement disguised as a gift, a Trojan horse of truly epic proportions.

## Magic to manic to toxic

As is becoming clear, the transition from magic to manic to toxic can be quite rapid with dramatic and detrimental, unintended consequences. Consider this for a moment: The pleasure and the magic of being able to share family vacation pictures easily via Flickr is obvious to hundreds of millions of people. Indeed, it was available long before iCloud, Dropbox, or Facebook (the biggest mania platform I can think of), which now allow sharing of my assets with even greater ease.

Yet Flickr can quickly become super-creepy when someone uses what I blissfully shared for my friends and family, taking my content entirely out of context and in total contradiction to its intended use.

For example, when, in 2015, the Dutch company Koppie-Koppie wanted to sell coffee mugs with cute baby pictures on them, they turned to Flickr to use freely available "Creative Commons (CC) licensed" family pictures as free models.[117] As long as you uploaded your pictures under the CC license, Flickr considers it fair use. Surprise, surprise. Most of the images' owners and their parents would beg to differ. No doubt, this is clearly a use of technology that runs contrary to its original intention. Unintended consequences can become pretty big, very fast, when amplified by networked technologies.

For some users, the magical sharing effect of Flickr was instantly destroyed by a different interpretation of usage permissions and by nefarious exploitation of unintended context—maybe not an illegal act per se, but certainly quite high on the creepiness scale. Koppie-Koppie is a great example of how quickly magic can become toxic.

## Unintended consequences will grow in exponential lockstep with the technologies that generate them

To be sure, Koppie-Koppie's case is probably a minor incident (unless it's your own kids' images being used) with little tangible damage being done. However, it does prompt the question: What if our large-scale participation in something that seems very benign, convenient, and beneficial to all enables it to become so vastly powerful that it develops its own purpose, its own reason for being, its own life? Facebook is the prime example here—which is why I have scaled back my use of it.

What if this increasingly powerful entity starts to infringe upon our more tacit or implicit privacy desires, yet is also so deeply embedded in our lives that we cannot do much about it? What if we are so immersed in this new medium that we start forgetting where we end and it starts?

What if an organization's technological ability and scope of intelligence became a thousand, a hundred thousand, or a million times as powerful as what we have today—as is the promise of quantum and cognitive computing, i.e. computers a million times faster than any box available today, and software that is not programmed but actually learns what it needs to do as it goes along?

What would be the unintended consequences of these developments? Would these new intermediaries and platforms eventually become more intentional in the use of our data in questionable ways in their quest to generate more revenues based on our participation, and to satisfy the financial expectations of their owners or the public markets? Given the almost complete absence of meaningful regulation for digital platforms, would such powerful organizations be able to resist the temptations to cross the line between unintended and planned misuse?

What makes us think this won't happen? We simply must consider these unpalatable what-ifs because this is the road we are on—fueled by exponential technologies. The power of social networks of the Web 2.0 era will look like child's play once we connect everyone and everything to a hugely powerful IoT in the cloud containing constantly learning and expanding AI systems like IBM's Watson or Google's DeepMind. Literally all our data, including our most personal medical and biological information, will become available, and we won't be able to blink without someone tracking it, both in reallife and the digital realm.

I believe technology and those that purvey it to will become exponentially and quite possibly infinitely better at figuring out exactly who we are, what we are thinking, and how to "play us"—at an ever lower cost. Hence, we will need to pay a lot more attention to where we end and where they start, i.e. where my humanity intersects with their technology—to the point of being inseparable.

In such a world, certain issues will certainly loom large. For example, how much will our perceptions be shaped by the filter bubble effect of only seeing or reading things that have been filtered for us, orchestrated by algorithms? How will we counter the risk of bias and manipulation due to the fact that we won't even know the logic behind what we will or will not see?

We should take this opportunity to start honing our skills of observing and challenging so that a more holistic stewardship can emerge. What will that mean for the expectations placed on politicians and government officials?

### Intelligent digital assistants and the cloud as extensions of ourselves

Today, we are already using simple machine intelligence in many instances, i.e. within mobile maps, email software, or dating apps. But while apps such as TripAdvisor can tell us what other people have thought about a restaurant we are considering, they don't know our entire culinary history from the past 20 years. They don't see inside our fridge, or monitor our toilet, as has been proposed as a new service in Japan,[118] and they don't connect all that information and compare it with 500 million other data points from other users that may be available right now. Nevertheless, TripAdvisor is already quite useful and has become a must-have for almost every restaurant and hotel. As little intelligence as it has, it's a useful tool if we don't ignore the context of its ratings and recommendations.

This rather mechanical, straightforward, yet already quite useful level of benign assistance is about to be dwarfed by rapid advances in the development of IDAs. This next generation of assistants will live primarily in the cloud rather than on our devices, and will track everything we do via our mobile gadgets, home automation systems, sensors, and computers. Just imagine the quantum power of IBM's Watson available to you via your mobile devices—and all you need to do is ask, without even touching a keyboard. Then, imagine all you need to do is think and issue a command via your BCI. Super-humanity is within reach.

In 2016 Siri, Google Now, and Cortana were already able to answer your simple questions about the weather or where to find something, and Gmail's AI answered some of your emails for you. Soon, they will be able to book most of your meetings or arrange your flights for you, without any need for supervision. The day after tomorrow, they will become your trusted friend in the sky. After that they may become as important as our own eyes and ears. After that, your guess is as good as mine, but the key question, again, is: Will they make us happy? And what is happiness, anyway (see chapter 9)?

In his 2015 article *"Is Cortana a Dangerous Step Towards Artificial Intelligence?"* the writer Brad Jones explains:

> AIs take on their own personalities, and grow more intelligent by collecting data and information from the world around them. However, that knowledge gradually fills up the available resources of the construct, and over time the AI will become rampant. An AI in a state of rampancy thinks of humans as its inferior, developing a delusional sense of its own power and intellect.[119]

The key question will be whether those IDAs will be able to do things they were not specifically programmed for—and, as already discussed, this is exactly the promise of deep learning, i.e. a machine that can actually teach itself, a thinking machine that is learning rather than being programmed.

These extensions of ourselves will use the exponential powers of neural networks, deep learning, and cognitive computing to provide us with extremely powerful, personal, and highly anticipatory services.

In the process they will almost certainly develop pre-cognitive capabilities as well. Add AR/VR and BCIs to this mix and the sky may seem like a trivial limit for what future generations of IDAs might be capable of.

Once my IDA or bot knows my entire history, has access to all my real-time data, and can compare this with the data from hundreds of millions of other networked IDAs, it may very well be able to predict my actions and responses. Welcome to pre-crime, the idea of being able to prevent crimes because our bots would know when intent emerges, even if it would not be obvious to the person involved. The UK-based company Precobs already has such a software engaged in trials with local police forces.[120]

And welcome to the potential for global political manipulation via digital content and media networks, where my IDA will routinely represent me; or for all practical purposes, be me. Could my IDA fall victim to manipulation or deliberately collude to influence my decisions?

As research company Gartner put it back in 2013: Mobile devices sync me, see me, know me . . . and soon, they are me.[121] Again, I wonder: Will this lead to human flourishing? I seriously doubt it.

We may, someday quite soon, see our own IDA quarrel or negotiate with the airline reservation system's IDA to get the best possible deal for our flight to Hawaii within the next six minutes. And of course, most shopping will no longer be done by us—our IDA will be much quicker and more efficient, constantly collecting coupons and sales announcements, and making situation-aware decisions at lightning-fast pace. All I need to do is think about a purchase and . . . it's already queued up for me. Instant satisfaction in a world of total abundance. But while we are certain to have total abundance on the outside, we are also certain to have increasing scarcity on the inside, i.e. in relationships, community, values, spirituality, and beliefs.

Believe it or not, for many pundits and the techno-determinists in Silicon Valley, the near-future powers of IDAs still sound rather benign—it's no big deal to use an IDA when it's just a little bit better than what my app does today, right?

Well, let's look at some scenarios that would be more on the creepy side, yet represent a distinct possibility in the medium-term future.

Let's first consider that in order to be brilliant, fast, anticipatory, and intuitive, my IDA—this shiny engine and extension of myself, my personal cloud robot—would have to have a huge amount of information about me. Well, actually, it might well need to know absolutely everything about me, culling real-time information from every available source and constantly updating it. And many of us would likely feel that we would want such a system to have all these details about us. This would allow the quality of the service we receive to be improved constantly, making our lives even easier—indeed a seemingly small price to pay for that amazing convenience and much-increased personal power.

Opting-in to be constantly tracked, monitored, and nudged is where it all starts, and the widely used "share this" or "save this" as favorite functionalities are only two examples of how we get lured into constantly staying connected to platforms. Google is the absolute master at this, keeping us inside its ever-expanding universe at all times—and Google is just one example of many large global platforms that want to become a kind of global brain that duplicates every single user in the cloud. Tracking us in such a way is money in the bank for companies for whom data is indeed the new oil, especially for global platforms such as Google, Baidu, Alibaba, and Facebook that don't really sell anything physical but serve largely as data-miners, advertising engines, and information super-nodes. Imagine this concept amplified a thousandfold by the IoT and AI, and you can hear their cash registers "ka-ching!" with delight.

### Total tracking, anyone?

So what could possibly go wrong with IDAs? Here are some examples of how they could fail us:

- **Significantly amplified security risks and privacy implications:** Your IDA may be hacked, tricked, pressured, or bribed into divulging some or all of your information to other

AIs it encounters online. For example, it might be tricked into giving away the passwords that allow it to send emails, make purchases, and access social media channels on your behalf. The depth of such amalgamated information leakages could be so huge that it could cause irreparable damage to you—and you may not even be aware that your IDA has become corrupted!

- **Exponential surveillance:** Your IDA would act like a 24/7/365 recorder of your life in digital and meatspace, aka real life, alike. Anyone with the right credentials or enough authority, fake or otherwise, could access your data. This would allow anyone with the right bot-hacking skills to profile you, or flag you as a suspect, a dissenter, or as a dangerous individual. They could use unconnected or out-of-context bits of information to frame or manipulate you. Imagine if the amount of data your bot could access were to become a thousandfold deeper and smarter because it could correlate your data with millions of other data feeds, for example on social networks. The results could dwarf even the most dystopian projections of George Orwell.

  Hence, the untempered cloud-bot/IDA scenario strikes me as an open invitation for willy-nilly abuse and persecution, especially in those countries that already have no real privacy protection, or have already shown their disregard for the basic privacy rights of their citizens. The other point to consider is that our governments may increasingly be able to access our IDAs and digital egos—legally, i.e. through the front door, or more covertly via a back door left open in the code. Consequently, it's safe to assume that every other serious hacker organization could do the same. I shudder to think what could happen if we all became digitally naked to such an extent.

- **Increased human deskilling:** Imagine that I used my IDA so much that I started forgetting or unlearning how to do things myself, for example, how to find my way in a strange city, how to find trustworthy information online, how to book a flight, how to run a spreadsheet, or even how to write by hand—a very distinct possibility. It stands to reason that I would quickly lose skills that used to be essential to being human, such as carrying on unmediated communications, regardless of the alleged slowness and potential errors that may allow for. Are we making humans increasingly replaceable? Should everything be automated just because we can?

- **Digiphrenia** (a great term coined by Douglas Rushkoff, whose books you need to read for sure):[122] One of the driving forces behind human deskilling by technology is our increasing desire to be able to be in several places at once. Technologies such as telepresence, messaging, and social media seem to allow this now, to some simulated degree, and all too often some of us are willing to give up authentic experiences in return.

To quote Douglas:

> Digiphrenia is really the experience of trying to exist in more than one incarnation of yourself at the same time. There's your Twitter profile, there's your Facebook profile, there's your email inbox. All of these sorts of multiple instances of you are operating simultaneously and in parallel. And that's not a really comfortable position for most human beings.[123]

- **Building relationships with screens and machines instead of with people:** Many tasks or processes that humans undertake frequently also inadvertently lead to building relationships with others, such as shopping for food or meeting team members to plan an event. Clearly, some of these interactions may not be essential or hugely valuable, for example, talking to a travel agent about booking a flight, or calling your banker about an investment option—both are things I never do, by the way.

So yes, some of these more minor tasks could be done by

machines without losing a truly human connection—I don't really need to make friends with my banker so that I can decide where to invest 5,000 euros. However, I think we need to consider whether to automate other, more involved human interactions such as visiting the doctor even if it's only to make sure we really only have a minor cold and not emphysema. In some cases, yes, it would be fine to just do your diagnosis from the comfort of your home; in other cases, it may dehumanize the doctor-patient relationship because the things that should not be automated or replaced by machines are those that actually create meaningful relationships.

Imagine automating a substantial part of your interactions with your staff or team members at work, as already proposed by startups such as x.ai with its automated assistant apps.[124] While there would be no harm in automating group-calendar entries based on an email, imagine if you received an email reply from a team member and did not know if was written by him or his IDA. Take it one stage further, how would you feel if a personal connection such as your father or mother was communicating to you via their IDA?

And where will this end? How far will we take this? Who defines where the AI stops and a human starts? Will the IDA end up inviting people to my next birthday party, ordering the food, choosing the music, collating a nice slideshow, and maybe even programming an ad-hoc website for the event? And will it then tell me how to be as happy as possible during my party? Would this be beneficial in building relationships between me and other humans, or would I be able to cut out some of the work only to lose the meaning? Will we build more relationships with machines because it's convenient?

- **Manipulation on an unimaginable scale is feasible and increasingly likely:** If we were to outsource our decisions to powerful IDAs, it would probably happen first with media and content; the basic functionalities are already in place within most social networks. Our IDAs could find and filter news, source movies, and sort our social media. The technology already pretty much influences or even decides what is best for us to see, read, or listen to. But a cloud-intelligence powered by exponential technologies would make today's offerings seem basic in comparison.

Imagine the possibility of just a handful of bots or leading IDA platforms controlling what billions of people get to see or pay attention to. Imagine what brands and advertisers would be willing to pay to be seen in the right place at the right time by exactly the right users.

The rise of IDAs raises some fundamental questions for me:

- What if this digital copy of me divulges information to the wrong people—such as my insurance company or the social security agency that may be in the process of approving or denying a benefit?
- What if my IDA became so much better at making most of my decisions for me that I followed its recommendations even when it's about making major life choices such as whom to marry, where to move, whether to have children, and how to educate them?
- What if my IDA filtered all the news and information in such a way that I would never come across a dissenting opinion again, and what if its logic could be manipulated by purchasing a campaign to influence me?

*"Gartner predicts that by year-end 2016, more complex purchase decisions such as back-to-school equipment made autonomously by digital assistants will reach $2 billion annually. This translates to roughly 2.5% of mobile users trusting assistants with $50 a year."*
*– "The World of Digital Assistants—Why Everyday AI Apps Will Make up the IoT"*[125]

The meteoric rise of IDAs will probably force me to update one of my favorite keynote quips: "Google knows more about us than our husband or wife." Having an IDA such as Google Now collecting millions of data points about me—such as location, browsing history, purchases, likes, emails, maps, and YouTube views—will certainly up the ante considerably. As I like to say, on the 100-point scale of what could be digitized, we are only at five. . . and we are already close to spinning out of control.

I keep coming back to the notion of "We ain't seen nothing yet." The meteoric rise of the IoT will bring yet another boost for the IDA platforms—generating ever more data to feed into the global brain that these systems will tap into. Increasingly, previously dumb pieces of hardware like drills, farming machines, pipelines, switches, and connectors are being fitted with sensors and wireless network connections. Pretty soon it will be possible to get live data from literally everything around us.

*"Social networks—the real kind, consisting of people you know and see in person and not on Facebook or Twitter—are as important to your health as exercise and diet, a new study finds. What's more, the number of social ties you have directly affects your health." –Charlie Sorrel, "Stop Being A Loner, It'll Kill You"*[126]

**So why are so few people concerned about this right now?**
There are many reasons why it may appear that so few critical voices comment on this shift from magic to manic to toxic. Here are three of them:

1. **Huge profits.** Connecting people, taking advantage of exponential technological progress, and providing cheap yet addictive mobile devices are probably among the biggest business opportunities ever. Purveying digital magic to people, aka the data economy, is bound to dwarf energy and transportation—and nobody wants to spoil this party.[127] In a society where profit and growth still rank supreme, manic

side effects and even toxic results are all too often considered externalities, not our problem.

2. **Lack of regulation and political ignorance.** Unlike the exploitation and supply of natural resources such as oil, gas, and water, there are very few global regulations that govern the application of AI, the addictive effects of technology, or the use of big data, i.e. the commercialization of our personal data on digital networks. This is a huge void that must be addressed.

3. **Addiction to technology ("mobile devices are the new cigarettes").** Exponential technologies that seem to make our lives easier, that play on our natural laziness and our need to be liked are highly addictive and often have a drug-like effect. Habits form very quickly—do you check your email one more time before going to bed, too? Do you feel "alone" when not connected to your favorite social network, and defenseless without Google maps or your messaging apps?

The bottom line is that selling magic and then upselling to manic or toxic is probably the biggest business opportunity of the Digital Age, and at its worst it's really no different than adding addictive substances to junk food or tobacco. As we progress exponentially, this strategy will need to be reviewed and probably curtailed if we want to end up with a society that actually pursues human happiness above all else.

### What technology wants: to go from second nature to nature

We sometimes use the phrase "this has become like second nature to me" to describe using tools or technologies that just feel natural. For example, people say, "Having my mobile phone always with me has become second nature," or, "Connecting with my friends on Facebook is second nature." This phrase describes something that has become a habit, something we do because it feels natural, we don't think about it anymore.

It has become second nature to like things on Facebook, to share images and videos on WhatsApp or other messaging apps, and to be constantly reachable on mobile devices. Google Maps is now second nature, and for an increasing number of Apple iPhone users, Siri is becoming second nature. Second nature is about doing something without much thought, an ingrained habit (almost like "natural" actions such as breathing) that we don't question anymore, something that we do automatically. In a good many cases, this is already borderline manic—how many times have you experienced the phantom-vibration syndrome, feeling a buzzing sensation in your pocket even though you left your mobile device at home?

But now, as we eagerly step into the vortex of exponential technological change, we can observe that an increasing number of technologies (or their vendors) are vying to become first nature, i.e. nature, period. Obviously a giant business opportunity. If being "just human" isn't good enough anymore or if being human is just too cumbersome, why not resort to technology to enhance or augment yourself? Why not make technology "first nature" and level the playing field between us and the machines?

The idea of human augmentation by technological means often falls squarely into the domain of businesses that want to monetize our desire to become more powerful, while making life easier for us. For a good many people, it's already becoming "first nature" to wear Fitbits and other health-tracking apps, wristbands, wearable computing devices, and sensors embedded in our jackets and shirts ("Of course I track all my vitals and monitor my body in such a way—that's just a natural thing to do"). The so-called quantified self is on the rise, everywhere, and entire new industries are being created around the concept. However, I often worry that these offerings may sooner or later turn us into quantified slaves or, even worse, into stupefied selves, effectively deskilling us by allowing us to outsource our thinking (and feeling) to external technologies.

Just imagine which other human augmentations could easily morph from nice-to-have, to second nature, to nature—because they simply would be too good to do without, and become virtually free and abundant. The list includes AR, VR, and holograms which enable me to project into a virtual space where I can interact with others as if I was actually there, as with Microsoft's HoloLens.[128] These tools could be very useful when visiting a museum, or for doctors doing surgery, or for firefighters entering an unknown building. But I think we should resist the drive for them to become second nature (never mind first nature).

Let's make no mistake about this: Many of these devices, services, and platforms—whether openly and intentionally or inadvertently—seek to diminish or completely eradicate the difference between us (human nature) and them (second nature), because achieving that would make them utterly indispensable and extremely valuable in commercial terms.

No longer could I be a healthy human being without using all those tracking devices and apps—I wonder how we ever even existed without them! Mission accomplished.

I maintain that we should not let technology move beyond that second-nature stage—indeed, much of that is already skating on thin ice. But technology that becomes nature (us) would mean that nature humanity becomes technology, as well—which is not a good path to human happiness, as I argue throughout this book.

This extract from a 2016 *Nature Institute* interview with author Stephen Talbott describes the challenge very well:

> Only if we counter these technologies with a greater power of attention to the specific, the qualitative, the local, the here and now, can we keep our balance. This is the general rule, first voiced, so far as I know, by Rudolf Steiner: To the extent we commit ourselves more fully to a machine-mediated existence, we must reach more determinedly toward the highest regions of our selves; otherwise, we will progressively lose our humanity.[129]

Our technology use is increasingly likely to go from magic to manic to toxic as exponential gains are achieved all around us. How often do we come away from an hour trawling the Internet or fiddling with a new app without remembering what we were seeking in the first place?

Going down the rabbit hole on an individual basis is one thing, but what if our society as a whole started living in it? And what uniquely human experiences are we already surrendering to the Internet, the mobile phone, the cloud, and our bots and intelligent assistants every day?

How can we spot the moments when boundaries are crossed between magic and manic? When or how does manic become toxic? And what will toxic be like when it is no longer a question of detoxing a single person but a whole culture? As *techne* becomes the who as well as the how, are we even strong enough and self-aware enough to wake ourselves?

# Chapter 7
# Digital Obesity: Our Latest Pandemic

*As we wallow and pig out on a glut of news, updates, and algorithmically engineered information that may be anything but, we entertain ourselves in a burgeoning tech-bubble of questionable entertainment.*

Obesity is a global issue, and, according to McKinsey, it's costing an estimated US$450 billion per year in the US alone, both in terms of healthcare costs and lost productivity.[130] The Centers for Disease Control and Prevention stated in 2015 that more than two-thirds of Americans are overweight, and an estimated 35.7% are obese.[131]

I believe we are reaching a similar or bigger challenge as we gorge on technology and bring on digital obesity.

I define digital obesity as a mental and technological condition in which data, information, media, and general digital connectedness are being accumulated to such an extent that they are certain to have a negative effect on health, well-being, happiness, and life in general.

Perhaps unsurprisingly, and despite those shocking health factoids, there is still little support globally for stricter regulation of the food industry to curb the use of addiction-building chemical additives, or to stop marketing campaigns that promote overconsumption. In America's never-ending war on drugs, harmful foodstuffs and sugars are never so much as hinted at. Just as organic foods now seem to be largely the preserve of the well-off and wealthy, so too can we expect anonymity and privacy to become expensive luxuries—out of reach for most citizens.

Consumers are buying gadgets and apps that will supposedly help them reduce food consumption and increase fitness, such as the Fitbit, Jawbone, Loseit, and now Hapifork—which alerts you by trembling if you eat too fast—very useful indeed.[132] It appears the idea is to buy (download) and consume yet another product or service that will miraculously, and without much effort, fix the original problem of overconsumption.

### Cravability means prosperity

The obvious bottom line is that the more people eat, the better it is for those who produce and sell our food—for example, growers, food processors, grocery stores, supermarkets, fast-food joints, restaurants, bars, and hotels. In addition, we may be shocked to find that, every year, every consumer in developed countries unwittingly ingests an estimated 150 pounds of additives—mostly sugar, yeast, and antioxidants, as well as truly nasty stuff such as MSG.[133] These substances are the lubricants of overconsumption. Not only do they make food prettier and more durable, they also make it taste better—as debatable as that is. Thus consumers are strung along by cleverly engineering a "need-for-more" so that it becomes very hard to find the exit from that kingdom of endless, happy consumption.

If this sounds like Facebook or your smartphone, you are getting my drift. The food industry actually calls this cravability or crave-ability.[134] In the world of technology, marketers call it magic, stickiness, indispensability, or more benignly, user engagement.

### Craving and addiction—tech's business model

Generating this kind of craving, or fueling our digital addictions in such a seemingly benign way, is clearly a powerful business model.[135] It is easy to apply the cravability concept to the leading social-local-mobile (SoLoMo) super-nodes such as Google and Facebook, or to platforms such as WhatsApp. Many of us literally crave connectivity as we conduct our daily lives, and when we disconnect we feel incomplete.

Yet somehow, I wonder if it really could be in the interest of big Internet firms that a large number of their users end up with digital obesity issues? Is that really in the best interests of the predominantly US-owned technology and Internet giants?[136] At the same time, we should not underestimate the strong temptation to make consumers dependent on these marvelous digital foods—to addict us to that serotonin-producing tsunami of likes, comments, and friend updates.

Think 2020 and imagine billions of hyperconnected consumers becoming digitally obese, hooked on a constant drip of information, media, and data—and their own feedback loops. This is a hugely tantalizing business opportunity that will far surpass the market for global food additives—projected by Transparency Market Research to be worth some US$28.2 billion by 2018.[137]

For a quick comparison of scale, the World Economic Forum estimates that the cumulative value of digitization could reach US$100 trillion over the next ten years. They suggest this underscores the opportunity to "create a promising future workforce where people and intelligent machines work together to improve how the world works and lives."[138] I admit that I like the idea but fail to see how we could still retain our humanity in such a highly machine-centric society.

### Whose responsibility is obesity?

Going back to food, you may ask: If the food industry makes so much money with their slightly (or more covertly) evil approach of addiction and cravability, why bother with those few consumers who can't seem to handle these temptations on their own? Isn't it simply their own fault and responsibility? Who would argue that anyone but the individual consumer should ultimately be responsible for handling their own food consumption? After all, it's a free world, and it's their own free will, right?

The problem is that in the coming era of exponentially increasing information and abundant connectivity, this laissez-faire strategy is unsustainable, precisely because we are only at the pivot on the exponential curve—the biggest shocks have yet to be seen!

The two key challenges are that firstly, digital food is mostly free or very cheap and even more ubiquitously available than physical food—it is distributed and instantly available at next to zero cost. Secondly, there are very few obvious side effects and physical warning signals. Most consumers won't understand what is happening or concern themselves with digital consumption and over-connectivity until it's a very obvious problem such as gaming addiction for teenagers in Korea.[139] Once you are obese it is very hard to reset your life to a different paradigm.

I believe we urgently need precise yet liquid public policies; new social contracts; global digital health standards; localized, responsive regulations; and deeper responsibility and involvement of marketers and advertisers. Technology providers need to (and I believe many already want to) support a balanced global manifesto of digital rights or digital health, consider proactive self-restraint, and switch to a more holistic business model that really does put people first. Hyperconnectivity above all is certainly not going to be our final destination, just like hyper-efficiency cannot be the sole purpose of business. Putting people first means putting our happiness first, and I would argue it's the only way to create lasting benefits in business as well as in society.

*"The difference between technology and slavery is that slaves are fully aware that they are not free" –Nassim Nicholas Taleb[140]*

### A tsunami of data is coming

As the amount of data, information, and media available grows exponentially, so a huge digital obesity challenge is now looming large. We need to take it seriously and tackle it because the digital strain will be even more crippling than physical obesity. There is already way too much communication and information in our lives (in fact, of course, it's infinite), and the paradox of choice is running wild all around us.[141]

We are presented with a fire hose of possibilities, all the time, anywhere, and they are way too tasty, too cheap, and too rich. Not a single day goes by without yet another service offering us more updates from our increasing number of friends; more ways to be disrupted by incessant notifications on pretty much any platform—witness the growing popularity of smartwatches, which are now selling more units than Swiss watches.[142] We are facing exponential growth in consumption options—more news; more music; more movies; more, better, and cheaper mobile devices; and seemingly total social connectivity.

We are drowning in a sea of apps—for dating, for divorces, for reporting potholes, even (as we have seen) for monitoring diapers.[143] We're under 24/7 assault from location-based alerts and communications such as iBeacons, digital coupons, new ways to send and receive messages at zero cost, 500 million tweets per day, [144] 400 hours of video uploaded to YouTube every minute, [145] and the list goes on and on. A veritable tsunami of input and it's dishing up abundance on the outside, but creating scarcity or a lack of meaning on the inside. In other words, we have increasingly more options at lower cost, but we are more worried about missing out, about "what we could have done"—all the time. Where is this going?

### Abundance outside, scarcity inside—bicycles for the mind or bullets for the soul?

We are bombarded with information input, and by and large we are pigging out as we once did at the US$9.99 all-you-can-eat Las Vegas buffets. The overlords of digital nourishment are of course the likes of Google and its Chinese counterparts Baidu and Alibaba. Google's genius lies in creating a seamless heaven (or at least a kingdom) of cross-consumption drawn from a huge number of very sticky and viral platforms such as Gmail, Google Maps, Google+, Google Now, YouTube, Android, and Google Search.

The Google universe is so hyper-efficient, so convenient, and so addictive that it is threatening to become utterly fattening for our brains, eyes, ears, and even our hearts and souls. I like to refer to this as the abundance outside/scarcity inside problem and as the bicycles for the mind or bullets for the soul dilemma: At the same time that our minds are gaining a kind of warp-speed because they are powered by Google et al., our arteries are clogged with all the junk that comes with these nonstop digital feasts, and our hearts are heavy with too many meaningless relationships and mediated connections that only exist on screens.

If indeed "Google knows me better than my wife," we must surely start to consider who is serving whom.[146] Is digital obesity designed into the system, is it more of a hidden agenda, or is it simply an unintended consequence of those very few entities that are now ruling our digital lives?

*"We become, neurologically, what we think" –Nicholas Carr*[147]

"The more a sufferer concentrates on his symptoms, the deeper those symptoms are etched into his neural circuits," writes Nicholas Carr in *What the Internet is Doing to Our Brains*:

> In the worst cases, the mind essentially trains itself to be sick. Many addictions, too, are reinforced by the strengthening of plastic pathways to the brain. Even very small doses of addictive drugs can dramatically alter the flow of neurotransmitters in a person's synapses, resulting in long-lasting alterations in brain circuitry and function. In some cases, the buildup of certain kinds of neurotransmitters, such as dopamine, a pleasure-producing cousin to adrenaline, seems to actually trigger the turning on or off of particular genes, bringing even stronger cravings for the drug. The vital path turns deadly.[148]

### New interfaces such as augmented and virtual reality add to the challenge

Achieving a balanced digital diet will become even harder as connectivity, devices, and applications become exponentially cheaper and faster, and as interfaces to information are reinvented. We'll go from reading or watching screens, to speaking to machines, to merely thinking to direct them. In short, we'll journey from GUI to NUI (graphical user interface to natural user interface).

At some point in the not-so-distant future we may have to consider the ultimate question: Do we now live inside the machine, or does the machine live inside of us?

### Data is the new oil: pay or become the content

It has been said many times before but it deserves repeating: Data is truly becoming the new oil. Those companies feeding off big data and the so-called networked society are swiftly becoming the next Exxon-Mobils, eagerly providing the new opium for the masses: digital food, total connectivity, powerful mobile devices, free content, Social, Local and Mobile (SoLoMo) superglue from the cloud via bots, and intelligent digital assistants (IDA). They provide the nourishment that we—the people formerly known as consumers—are in fact creating and sharing ourselves through our mere presence and participation.[149]

Yet most of us are getting very comfortable inside these beautifully walled gardens from Google, Facebook, Weibo, LinkedIn, and many others. We are consuming as much as we can while willingly becoming the food for others. As author Scott Gibson recently stated on the *Forbes* blog, "If you don't pay, you become the content."[150] We are stuffing each other in unprecedented ways, and much of it is incredibly enriching, satisfying, and addictive. But is this a Nirvana, a clever Faustian Bargain, or a recipe for disaster? Or does it all depend on who is doing the asking?

### The 2020 horizon for digital obesity

Cisco predicts that by 2020, 52% of the global population will be connected to the Internet—around four billion human users.[151] By then, every single piece of information, every picture, every video, every kernel of data, every location, and every uttering by every connected human is likely to be monitored, collected, connected, and refined into media, big data, and business intelligence. Artificial intelligence (AI) powered by quantum cognitive computers will generate mind-boggling insights from zettabytes (one sextillion $(10^{21})/2^{70}$ bytes) of real time data. Nothing will remain unobserved for very long.

Clearly, this could be heaven if you are a marketer, a vendor of the tools that handle those tasks, an over-eager government agency, or just a super-geek. Or it could be hell given the distinct possibility that the very same super-charged information will also enable perpetual global surveillance, as the Snowden revelations have made painfully obvious since 2013.[152]

Not only might we be obese with information, we will also be naked—not a pretty picture!

### No longer "if we can," but "if we should"
I predict the question of whether technology can do something will soon be replaced by the more relevant question of whether we should do what technology now affords us, and why. This is already true for many recent innovations and trends such as social media, the quantified self, Google Glass, 3D printing, or the supposedly imminent Singularity (see chapter 1).

Put in the context of digital obesity, the bottom line is this: Just because all of this media, data, knowledge, and even wisdom is becoming instantly and freely available, do we need to soak in it at all times? Do we really need an app to tell us where the music section is located; do we really need to cross-check our genomes before we go on a date; and do we really need to count our steps so that our fitness status can be updated on a social network?

### From "more is better" to "less is best"
Finally, it comes down to this: As with food, where obesity is more obvious, we urgently need to find a personal balance in our digital diet. We must define when, what, and how much information we connect to and eat. When must we reduce our intake, take time to digest, be in the moment, or even stay hungry? Yes, there is a real business opportunity here as well: Offline is the new luxury.

I believe that in the next few years, our digital consumption habits will transition from the traditional offline and Internet 1.0 "more is better" paradigm to the concept of "less is best." In striking that crucial balance between ignorant and omniscient—since neither extreme is desirable—we may want to take our lead from Albert Einstein, when he said, "Everything should be made as simple as possible, but not simpler."[153]

# Chapter 8
# Precaution vs. Proaction

*The safest and still most promising future is one where we do not postpone innovation, but neither do we dismiss the exponential risks it now involves as "somebody else's business."*

As technology's power increases exponentially, I believe it is critical to determine a sustainable balance between precaution and proaction. The former means looking proactively at what might happen—the possible consequences and unintended outcomes—before we proceed with a course of scientific exploration or technological development. In contrast, the proactionary approach advocates an attitude of moving ahead in the interest of progress before all the potential risks and ramifications are clear.

Should we restrain science, inventors, and entrepreneurs if the resulting inventions are likely to have a materially adverse impact on humanity? Absolutely. Should we stall or prohibit scientific leaps that might be mostly beneficial to society but would need regulation to achieve a balanced outcome? Absolutely not. Indeed, prohibiting such advances might not even be possible.

The answer, of course, will be in a wise and holistic balance between these two positions, once again requiring us to become better future stewards.

Let's explore both positions in more detail.

Initially born out of environmental considerations, the precautionary principle holds that those who create things with potentially catastrophic consequences must not be allowed to proceed until they have proven that any unintended consequence can indeed be controlled. In other words, the burden to prove that a venture isn't harmful falls on those who want to undertake it.

This principle was applied in recombinant DNA research (the Asilomar conference) and its interpretation directly impacted the work done on the Large Hadron Collider at CERN (Switzerland) to address concerns that it may inadvertently generate a black hole.[154] [155] As in the case of the Large Hadron Collider, collective caution over technological developments must obviously trump potentially disastrous innovation that may create existential risks for humanity. The Wingspread Declaration (1999) summarizes the precautionary principle as follows:

> When an activity raises threats of harm to human health or the environment, precautionary measures should be taken even if some cause and effect relationships are not established scientifically. In this context, the proponent of the activity, rather than the public, should bear the burden of proof.[156]

The Rio Declaration of 1992 presented an even stronger clause: "Where there are threats of serious or irreversible damage, lack of full scientific certainty shall not be used as a reason for postponing cost-effective measures."[157]

I think that both of these statements could still hold true when looking at Artificial Intelligence (AI), machine intelligence, autonomous systems, human genome editing, and geo-engineering.

In contrast, the proactionary principle argues that humanity has always invented technology, and has always taken many risks doing so. We should therefore not add undue restraints to what people can or cannot invent. In addition, this principle stipulates that we should account both for the cost of potential restrictions and for the costs of foregone opportunities.

The proactionary principle was introduced by transhumanist philosopher Max More[158] and further articulated by UK sociologist

Steve Fuller.[159] Since the very idea of transhumanism is based on the concept of transcending our biology, i.e. the possibility of becoming at least part machine, uninhibited proactivity is naturally part of the story—no surprise there.

## A thoughtful and humanist balance

Here is what I am proposing: Too much precaution may paralyze us with fear and create a self-amplifying cycle of restraint. Pushing cutting-edge science, technology, engineering and math (STEM) activities or game-changing inventions into the underground will quite likely criminalize those undertaking them. That is obviously not a good response to the problem because we might actually discover things that would be our human duty to investigate further, such as the possibility of ending cancer. The things that make humanity flourish obligate us to set them free.

However, a purely proactionary approach won't work for us, either, because there is just too much at stake given the exponential, combinatorial, and interdependent nature of technological advances we are now experiencing. One fears it is almost certain that technology will eventually trump humanity if we merely follow the proactive approach as set forth today. Just as too much precaution will stifle progress and innovation, too much proactivity will free some powerful and likely uncontrollable forces that we should keep locked up for the time being.

As always, our challenge will be to find and keep that balance—between Pandora's Box and Aladdin's lamp.

We are on an exponential and combinatorial path in many STEM-related disciplines. Many traditional safeguarding approaches will prove to be useless, because the speed of change and the magnitude of potential unintended consequences have been increasing so dramatically ever since we reached the inflection of the curve in 2016, when we started increasing from four to eight (not five) and took that very first really big step.

An approach that worked just fine when we were doubling from 0.01 to 0.02 or even from one to two may no longer be appropriate when we are doubling successively from four up to 128—the stakes are just so much higher, and the consequences are so much harder for human minds to understand.

Imagine the consequences of being too proactive with AI, geo-engineering, or human genome editing. Imagine entering an arms race with AI-controlled weapons that can kill without human supervision. Imagine rogue nations and nonstate actors experimenting with controlling the weather and causing permanent damage to the atmosphere. Imagine a research lab in a not-so-transparent country coming up with a formula to program superhumans.

In his book, *Our Final Invention: Artificial Intelligence and the End of the Human Era,* author James Barrat provides a good summary of this dilemma:

> We don't want an AI that meets our short-term goals—please save us from hunger—with solutions detrimental in the long term—by roasting every chicken on earth—or with solutions to which we'd object—by killing us after our next meal.[160]

There is simply too much at stake to proceed with utter and unrestrained technological enthusiasm, or to merely say that it's inevitable or our destiny.

It is worth reading transhumanist Max More's original declaration on this topic in 2005:

> The precautionary principle, while well-intended by many of its proponents, inherently biases decision-making institutions toward the status quo, and reflects a reactive, excessively pessimistic view of technological progress. By contrast, the proactionary principle urges all parties to actively take into account all the consequences of an activity—good as well as bad—while apportioning precautionary measures to the real threats we face.

While precaution itself implies using foresight to anticipate and prepare for possible threats, the principle that has formed around it threatens human well-being. The precautionary principle has become enshrined in many international environmental treaties and regulations, making it urgent to offer an alternative principle and set of criteria. The need for the proactionary principle will become clear if we understand the flaws of the precautionary principle.[161]

On the one hand, I cannot really disagree with much of More's argument, especially given my past Silicon Valley experiences as an Internet entrepreneur trying to push ahead with innovation. But then again, Max wrote this in 2005—some ten years before we reached the pivot point of exponential technologies. What may have sounded reasonable but slightly techno-centric back then could lead to dangerous decisions today. Do you really want your future determined by nontransparent and unaccountable governments, the rulers of Silicon Valley, greedy venture capitalists, or military organizations such as the US Defense Advanced Research Projects Agency (DARPA)?

# Chapter 9
# Taking the Happenstance out of Happiness

*As big tech simulates quick hits of hedonistic pleasure, how can we protect the deeper forms of happiness that involve empathy, compassion, and consciousness?*

**Happiness:** Good fortune or luck in life or in a particular affair; success, prosperity
**Happenstance:** A chance event; a coincidence
—*The Oxford English Dictionary*

### Just what is happiness?

Throughout this book I argue that pursuit of maximum human happiness should be a primary purpose of technological progress. Striving for happiness is an essential component of being human—uniting us all. Just as we all have ethics (though not necessarily religion), the pursuit of happiness is a universal imperative shared by all humans, regardless of culture or belief system.

We are all engaged in the constant pursuit of happiness throughout our lives. Our daily decisions are driven by this impulse to create enjoyable or fulfilling experiences, whether indulging in momentary pleasure, delaying gratification in the service of a longer-term benefit, or pursuing higher fulfillment beyond the basic needs of food and shelter.

As we face the coming convergence of man and machine, I think it's essential that we don't confuse luck with happiness. Luck is more accidental, while happiness is a question of designing the right framework.

I strongly believe we must put the pursuit of happiness and human flourishing at the center of this man-machine debate. What purpose would technology serve if it does not further human flourishing? And yes, I think it is possible for us to design our future in such a way that we don't just depend on luck, but rather create the best possible circumstances for happiness (more on that later).

Trying to define happiness can be a murky proposition, as it's an abstract and subjective concept. Wikipedia defines it as follows:

> Happiness, gladness, or joy is a mental or emotional state of well-being defined by positive or pleasant emotions ranging from contentment to intense joy.[162]

When I started researching what happiness actually is, I repeatedly ran across a distinction between two different types of happiness. The first, hedonic happiness, is a positive mental high point, usually temporary, and often described as pleasure. It may be fleeting, it may be momentary, and it often leads us into habits. For example, some of our hedonic pleasures can lead to addictions such as food, alcohol, and smoking. Social networks such as Facebook have often been described as a "pleasure trap," a mechanism for hedonistic self-presentation and pleasure facilitation.

The second type of happiness is known as eudaimonic happiness, a kind of deeper happiness and contentment. Wikipedia explains *eudaimonia* (or the Anglicized version, eudaemonia, which I will use in this book) as follows: "*Eudaimonia* is a Greek word commonly translated as happiness or welfare."[163] "Human flourishing" is another popular meaning of eudaemonia and may serve as a more accurate terminology for the purpose of this book.

When I was a student of Lutheran theology in Bonn in the early 1980s (surprised?), I was deeply immersed in the teachings of the ancient Greek philosopher Aristotle. He was referring to eudaemonia when he wrote some 2,300 years ago that, "happiness is the meaning and the purpose of life, the whole aim and end of human existence." Eudaemonia is, of course, a central concept within Aristotelian philosophy, along with the terms *aretē* (virtue or excellence) and *phronesis* (practical or ethical wisdom).

*Eudaemonia*, *aretē*, and *phronesis*—if you'll pardon my Greek— have since become constant objectives in my work, and I think they are the key to understanding which path humanity should take as it is being steamrolled—or should we say "steam-punked"—by exponential technological change. In other words, we are already lost in a place humanity has never been before. However, there are ancient threads of wisdom (as above) that may yet serve us to escape this technology-centric maze in which we increasingly find ourselves.

## What makes us happy?

If human flourishing simply meant a more pleasurable life, better and more efficient business, more profit, and steady growth fueled by technology, then, by all means, let's agree to use machines and algorithms to achieve that. And for a while—as we spiral towards inevitable hyper-efficiency and what will likely be capitalism-crushing abundance—that may work just fine.

## GDP, GNH, or GPI: honest criteria of happiness?

If we define *flourish* too narrowly, mostly in economic or financial terms, we will end up with outdated definitions such as Gross Domestic Product (GDP) and Gross National Product (GNP) rather than a more inclusive measure such as Gross National Happiness (GNH).

GNH is a term originally coined in the 1970s in Bhutan (a country which I had a chance to visit right before the completion of this book). It means applying a much wider, more holistic, ecosystemic approach when measuring the state of a nation. Sometimes put in the context of political happiness, GNH is based on traditional Buddhist values rather than the traditional Western values that GDP or GNP usually reference—indicators such as economic growth, investment output, return on investment, and employment. The four pillars of GNH philosophy reflect this dramatically different underlying philosophy: sustainable development, preservation and promotion of cultural values, conservation of the natural environment, and establishment of good governance.[164]

Similarly, when it comes to making future decisions about the relationship between technology and humanity, I find GNH to be a very interesting, parallel approach because it puts happiness squarely in the center of measuring progress and value. Economic factors should not overshadow happiness-related issues—an obvious criterion—and efficiency should never become more important than humanity—which is one of my ten key rules at the end of this book.

Another way to measure the success of nations is the Genuine Progress Indicator (GPI), which assesses 26 variables related to economic, social, and environmental progress.[165] GPI is valuable because it takes externalities into full account. The consequences are part of the equation, which is very much what I would propose when addressing the unintended consequences of technology. GPI's economic indicators include inequality and the cost of unemployment; environmental indicators include the cost of pollution, climate change, and nonrenewable energy resources; while social indicators include the value of housework, higher education, and volunteer work.

What would happen if we applied a combination of GPI and GNH to achieve a more human-centric measurement of progress? This question will be important because if we continue to measure the wrong things, then we will most likely also continue to *do* the wrong thing. That would be a cardinal mistake in this age of exponential technological progress. First, the resulting errors would have infinitely larger unintended consequences, and second, doing so would once again give way too much power to technology and way too little to humans.

If all we measure is the hard data any given action produces, such as how many sales a certain employee has made, then our conclusions would be seriously biased as well. In practice, none of the uniquely human factors are that simple to measure—such as how many relationships with key clients that person may have, and whether he feels compassion with their issues and challenges. The more we pretend our data (and the artificial intelligence (AI) that learns from it) is 100% complete in a truly human way, the more misguided the system's conclusions. We tend to ignore androrithms in favor of algorithms because we like shortcuts and simplifications.

Measuring how much more efficient a business or a country could be because of digitization and automation might paint a very promising economic picture. However, measuring how happy its employees or citizens would be after everything is automated and robotized might present a very different social perspective.

Back in 1968, US Senator Robert Kennedy was already flagging GDP as an ill-guided metric which "measures everything except that which makes life worthwhile."[166] For me, this highlights a critical point: Algorithms can measure or even simulate everything except for what really matters to humans. Having said that, I don't mean to belittle what algorithms and technology in general can do for us. I just think it's important to put technology in its place, i.e. to engage where it's appropriate and to disengage where it's detrimental.

## Misdefining what human flourishing means will only empower machines

My concern is that we will only realize belatedly that we have misdefined flourishing for too long. We have accepted hedonic pleasures as good enough because they can often be manufactured, organized, or provided by technology. Social networks offer a great example: We can indeed experience the pleasure of being liked by others—which is, let's face it, a kind of hedonism. . . a digital pleasure trap. But we are not likely to experience the happiness of a meaningful and personal human contact (in Martin Seligman's PERMA kind of way, a key term that I will outline below).[167]

Maybe we will only truly understand the difference at that final point when every single feature that makes us human has either been replaced or made near impossible by hyper-efficient and compliance-enforcing technology, when we've forgotten or lost the skills to make anything work on our own. I certainly hope not, but faced with these exponential technological changes, it is clear that we need to start defining "flourishing" as growing in a healthy way. This means developing a more holistic view of our future, one that looks beyond the merely mechanistic, reductionist, and often hedonistic happiness approaches favored by so many technologists.

The psychologist Martin Seligman states that true happiness isn't solely derived from external, momentary pleasures. He uses the PERMA framework to summarize the key findings from his research on positive psychology.[168] In particular, humans seem happiest when they have:

- Pleasure (tasty food, warm baths)
- Engagement (or flow, the absorption within an enjoyed yet challenging activity)
- Relationships (social ties have turned out to be an extremely reliable indicator of happiness)
- Meaning (a perceived quest or belonging to something bigger)
- Accomplishments (having realized tangible goals).

Technology may indeed offer significant value in enabling Pleasure and Accomplishments and possibly contributing to Engagement. In contrast, I don't believe technology will be of material help in furthering real Relationships, or in establishing sense, purpose, or Meaning. In fact, quite the opposite may be true, as technology can often be quite corrosive to relationships, as when we obsess with our mobile devices at a family dinner.

Technology can muddle meaning and purpose (caused by data overload and careless automation), lead to more extreme filter bubbles (feeding us only that content we seemingly like), and facilitate further media manipulation. Sure, technology—as a tool not as a purpose—is and will be helpful across the board—but once we go further up the exponential scale, the overuse of and dependency upon it might well be equally detrimental.

I often wonder what will happen once exponential technologies really kick in. Will our lives become more hedonistic or more eudaemonic—more hit-driven or more deeply meaningful? Will we fall prey to even shallower pleasures where machines govern and mediate our experience, or will we strive for happiness that is uniquely human?

### Compassion—a unique trait connected to happiness

An important human factor to consider in this context is compassion. In his 2015 book, *An Appeal by the Dalai Lama to the World: Ethics Are More Important than Religion,* the Dalai Lama speaks about the relationship between happiness and compassion:

> If we want to be happy ourselves, we should practice compassion, and if we want other people to be happy, we should likewise practice compassion.[169]

Compassion—simply put as "the sympathetic concern for the sufferings or misfortunes of others"—is one of the hardest things to grasp, and certainly one of the hardest to practice. Compassion is much harder than cleverness and intellectual prowess.

Can you imagine a computer, an app, a robot, or a software product that has compassion? A machine that feels what you feel, that resonates with your emotions, and that suffers when you suffer? Sure, we can foresee machines that can understand emotions or even read compassion in human faces and body language. We can also imagine machines that would be capable of simulating human emotions, simply by copying or learning from what we do and therefore appearing to be actually feeling things.

However, the key difference is that machines will never have a sense of being. They cannot be compassionate, they can only ever hope to simulate it well. This is surely a critical distinction we should reflect on in greater detail when we consider the technological tsunamis rushing to swallow us. If we further confused a well-executed simulation with actual being, mistaking an algorithmic version of sentience with actual consciousness, we would be in deep trouble. That confusion is also the central flaw of transhumanism.

In my view, machines will become extremely good, fast, and cheap at simulating or duplicating human traits, but they will never actually be human. The real challenge for us, will be to resist the temptation to accept these simulations as "good enough" and allow them to replace uniquely human interactions. It would be a foolish and dangerous move to forsake a truly human eudaemonia experience for the ubiquitously available and quick-hit hedonic pleasures provided by machines.

In *Our Final Invention: Artificial Intelligence and the End of the Human Era,* James Barrat writes:

> A powerful AI system tasked with ensuring your safety might imprison you at home. If you asked for happiness, it might hook you up to a life support and ceaselessly stimulate your brain's pleasure centers. If you don't provide the AI with a very big library of preferred behaviors or an ironclad means for it to deduce what behavior you prefer, you'll be stuck with whatever it comes up with. And since it's a highly complex system, you may never understand it well enough to make sure you've got it right.[170]

### Happiness vs. money: experiences vs. possessions

People often point out that happiness based on material belongings or financial standing is actually rather limited in importance. Research has shown that in so-called developed countries, overall happiness does increase when people make more money but only to a certain point: Different studies suggest that anything beyond US$50,000–75,000 per year does not really add much extra happiness to people's lives. The correlation between income and well-being slopes off.[171]

Happiness cannot be acquired or purchased, and therefore would be impossible to stuff into an app, a bot, or some other machine. Supporting evidence suggests that experiences have a much longer impact on our overall happiness than possessions.[172] Experiences are personal, contextual, timely, and embodied. Experiences are based on those unique qualities that make us human—our androrithms.

As noted in the *Huffington Post* blog in April 2015 by Dr. Janxin Leu, director of product innovation at HopeLab:

> Scholars at the University of Virginia, University of British Columbia, and Harvard University released a study in 2011 after examining numerous academic papers in response to an apparent contradiction: When asked to take stock of their lives, people with more money report being a good deal more satisfied. But when asked how happy they are at the moment, people with more money are barely different than those with less.[173]

## Human happiness is—or should be—the primary purpose of technology

Technology, derived from the Greek words *techne* (method, tool, skill, or craft) and *logia* (knowledge, from the gods), has always been created by humans to improve their well-being, but now it seems likely that soon technology will be used to improve humans themselves.

We used to create technology to improve our life conditions in a way that made spontaneous happiness more likely and more prevalent. For example, Skype, GoogleTalk, and all kinds of messaging apps allow us to connect to pretty much anyone, anytime, anywhere, and all for free. Now, however, due to exponential and combinatorial technological progress, technology increasingly becomes a purpose in and of itself. We find ourselves trying to get more Facebook "likes", or constantly having to react to notifications and prompts because the system demands attention.

What if the tool becomes the meaning—as has already happened with Facebook? What if they are so irresistible and so convenient that we give them their own purposefulness? When will those smartphones and smart-screens, smartwatches, and virtual reality (VR) glasses become cognitive themselves and go beyond merely being our tools? What if our external brains can connect directly to our own neocortex?

### Technology has no ethics—and lives in a cloud of nihilism—a space without beliefs

As much as most of us love technology, we now need to face the fact that it does not have, nor will it ever have, nor should it have, any inherent consideration for our values, beliefs, and ethics. It will only consider our values as data feeds explaining our behavior.

Bots and intelligent digital assistants (IDA) will increasingly vacuum up, read, and analyze tens of millions of data feeds about me, and chew on every digital breadcrumb I drop. However, no matter how much "Gerd data" they gather and analyze, software and machines will never truly comprehend my values or ethics, because they cannot be human in the same way that I am. They will always be approximations, simulations, and simplifications. Useful—yes. Real—no.

Let me give you some examples of the ethical challenges posed by technology advances.

Many nuclear scientists did not envision the creation of the atomic bomb when they first worked on the underlying scientific and mathematical challenges. Einstein considered himself a pacifist but still encouraged the US government to build the bomb before Hitler would. As stated earlier, J. Robert Oppenheimer, widely seen as the father of the atomic bomb, lamented his actions after Hiroshima and Nagasaki.[174] Yet, the ethics of the military and political complex in which they operated effectively made both of them contributors to weapons of mass destruction.

The Internet of Things (IoT) is another great example—it is certain to be of great benefit in collecting, connecting, and combining vast amounts of data from hundreds of billions of web-connected objects. Hence, it could be a potential solution to many global challenges, such as climate change and environmental monitoring.

The idea is that once everything is smart and connected, we can make many processes more efficient, cut costs, and achieve big gains in protecting the environment. While these are clever ideas, the current schemes for realizing the IoT are almost completely void of attention to human considerations, androrithms, and ethical concerns. It is totally unclear how privacy will be maintained in this global-brain-in-the-cloud, how total surveillance will be prevented, and who will be in charge of all this new data. Right now the focus is very much on the wonders of efficiency and hyperconnectivity, while the unintended consequences and negative externalities don't seem to be anybody's concern.

In healthcare, Silicon Valley exponential abundance expert Peter Diamandis (whose work I generally appreciate a lot) talks in positive terms about Human Longevity, Inc., his new startup created with genetics pioneer Craig Venter, and how it will enable us to live much longer—possibly forever.[175] However, he seems to largely ignore most ethical or moral issues that surround the debate around aging, longevity, and death.

Who will be able to afford these treatments? Will only the rich live to be 100-plus? What would it mean to end death? Is death really a disease, as Diamandis says, or is it an integral and unchangeable part of being human? Questions abound, but, much like the early days of nuclear weapons research, many of Silicon Valley's technologists seem to be proceeding as fast and as far as they can without a modicum of reflection on what issues their innovations may end up causing.

> *"Death is a great tragedy . . . a profound loss. . . I don't accept it . . . I think people are kidding themselves when they say they are comfortable with death." –Ray Kurzweil*[176]

The key message here is that technology, like money, is neither good nor bad. It merely exists as a means. In the 1950s, Octavio Paz, the great Mexican poet, summarized it well:

> The nihilism of technology lies not only in the fact that it is the most perfect expression of the will to power but also in the fact that it lacks meaning. "Why?" and "To what purpose?" are questions that technology does not ask itself.[177]

I wonder if the nihilism of exponential technologies would be exponential as well? A thousand times as nihilistic, and maybe equally narcissistic? Will we eventually be a species completely devoid of consciousness, mystery, spirituality, and soul, simply because there's no room for these androrithms in this coming machine age?

Two things are critical to consider in this context:

1. Really great technology should always be designed to further human happiness first and foremost, i.e. not simply result in growth and profit because just striving for exponential growth and profit is very likely to turn us into machines before too long. This new paradigm will represent a dramatic shift for every business and organization.
2. Technology with potentially catastrophic consequences—such as geo-engineering or artificial general intelligence—should be guided and supervised by those who have proven to possess practical wisdom—what the ancient Greeks called *phronesis*. Stewardship of these technologies should not be placed in the hands of technology developers, corporations, military bureaucrats, venture capitalists, or the world's largest Internet platforms.

What will all the technological progress amount to if we as a species do not flourish, if we do not achieve something that genuinely lifts all of us onto another plane of happiness?

Consequently, when evaluating new technologies or the latest wave of science, technology, engineering and math (STEM) advances, we should always ask whether or not a particular innovation will actually further the collective well-being of most parties involved in realizing it.

Will cheaper and faster technologies, more convenience, more abundance, easier consumption, superhuman powers, or further economic gains really make us happy? Will better apps, bots, IDAs, powerful augmented reality (AR) and virtual reality (VR), or instant access to a global brain via a new brain-computer-interface (BCI) really mean that we, as a species and individually, will truly flourish? Or will it be primarily those who create, own, and offer the tools and platforms that will reap the rewards?

## Human well-being should be the goal

Particularly when discussing the future of technology, I feel that well-being—the state of being comfortable, healthy, or happy—is becoming the key word. Well-being implies a more holistic approach that goes way beyond measuring our body functions, our mental computing power, or the number of synapses in our brains. It expresses embodiment, context, timeliness, connectedness, emotions, spirituality, and a thousand other things we have yet to explain or even understand. Well-being isn't algorithmic—it is androrithmic, based on complex things such as trust, compassion, emotion, and intuition.

Technology is often very good at creating great so-called well moments such as being able to call a loved one anywhere and anytime I want. However, well-being is something that transcends technological facilitation to a very large degree. Having immersed myself in Internet entrepreneurship and dabbled with digital music startups for almost ten years, it was only after the sudden demise of my dotcom enterprise back in 2002 that I learned how a more holistic well-being really comes from relationships, from meaning, from purpose, and from context. Happiness cannot be automated!

## Can technology manufacture happiness?

Exponential technologies such as AI will undoubtedly attempt to create the conditions in which human happiness or even well-being can be furthered. Some will also actively seek to manufacture it for us—or at least, a digital approximation of it. Increasingly, we are seeing arguments that happiness can be programmed or otherwise organized or orchestrated by super-smart technology. The key argument of the techno-progressive thinkers is that being happy is just the result of the right kinds of neurons firing at the right time, in the right order. They reason that it's all just biology, chemistry, and physics and can thus be understood, learned, and copied completely by computers.

> *"We are looking at a society increasingly dependent on machines, yet decreasingly capable of making or even using them effectively." –Douglas Rushkoff,* Program or Be Programmed: Ten Commands for a Digital Age[178]

Maybe we can create a kind of happiness machine that would manipulate, control, and program us and our environment. Maybe there is an app for that—or at least there should be! Take a look at *www.happify.com* to see how the idea of organizing happiness is already being marketed—a software tool that teaches you happiness! One can only imagine how this could turn out by 2025—an app that connects directly to our brain via a BCI or via tiny implants to make sure we are happy all the time, and—critically—that we consume happiness all the time!

It sometimes seems to me that the entrepreneurs pursuing these exploits think that human emotions, values, and beliefs should be subject to even more exponential advances in STEM. The rationale seems to be that once we get far enough down this path, all of it will be subject to programming by us, including (you guessed it) ourselves. Then, we can finally rid ourselves of our biological constraints and become truly universal beings—I can't wait!

### Mood bots and tech pleasures

Technology is already able to create, program, or manipulate pleasurable moments (i.e. hedonic happiness) for us, and this is a business that will certainly boom in the near future. This already happens on the Facebook newsfeed, which displays only those items that will make you feel good and liked. It's happening in e-commerce with shopping sites that employ hordes of neuroscientists to fine-tune new digital instant-satisfaction mechanisms. It's being done in healthcare with nootropics (so-called smart drugs and cognitive enhancers) that are supposed to give you a kick of super-mental capabilities.

And soon, it will be done via very skillful manipulation of our senses through the voice- and gesture-controlled (not typed) conversations that we'll have with our omnipresent digital assistants. It will also take place via AR/VR devices such as Facebook's Oculus Rift and new kinds of human-computer interfaces and neural implants. Computers will try to make us feel happy. They will try to be our friends. And they'll want us to love them.

And it will only get worse (or better, depending on your viewpoint).

A September 2015 article by Adam Piore in the *Nautilus* journal highlights how these mood bots might function:

> James J. Hughes, a sociologist, author, and futurist at Hartford's Trinity College, envisions a day not too far from now when we will unravel the genetic determinants of key neurotransmitters like serotonin, dopamine, and oxytocin, and be able to manipulate happiness genes—if not serotonin-related 5-HTTLPR then something like it—with precise nanoscale technologies that marry robotics and traditional pharmacology. These "mood bots," once ingested, will travel directly to specific areas of the brain, flip on genes, and manually turn up or down our happiness set point, coloring the way we experience circumstances around us.
>
> "As nanotechnology becomes more precise, we're going to be able to affect mood in increasingly precise ways in ordinary people," says Hughes, who also serves as executive director of the Institute for Ethics and Emerging Technologies, and authored the 2004 book *Citizen Cyborg: Why Democratic Societies Must Respond to the Redesigned Human of the Future.*[179]

I would argue that digital technology has already become pretty good at furnishing hedonic pleasures to its users. Just think about apps, personal digital assistants, and social media in general, where the entire purpose of connecting with others is often reduced to getting a quick dopamine boost based on the responses of complete strangers.

In a way, social networks are already pretty amazing "hedonistic happiness generators."

But of course, the key question is what could exponential technological gains possibly do to furnish or even support eudaemonia (happiness as the meaning and the purpose of life, as the aim of human existence), or support our striving towards a noble purpose, or discovering the meaning of life? This strikes me as mission impossible simply because technology does not ask about—or concern itself with—purpose at all. And why should it?

Then, there is the question of whether such eudaemonian happiness can be planned, orchestrated, or pre-arranged at all, digital or not. This is a concept which Viktor Frankl, the Austrian psychologist and founder of logo-therapy, explores in his 1946 book *Man's Search for Meaning*:

> Happiness cannot be pursued; it must ensue, and it only does so as the unintended side effect of one's personal dedication to a cause greater than oneself or as the by-product of one's surrender to a person other than oneself. The more a man tries to demonstrate his sexual potency or a woman her ability to experience orgasm, the less they are able to succeed. Pleasure is, and must remain, a side-effect or by-product, and is destroyed and spoiled to the degree to which it is made a goal in itself.[180]

The idea that hedonic pleasures are a side-product of a larger flourishing (eudaemonia) makes a lot of sense to me. Hence, my argument that we should embrace technology—experience the pleasure of it—but not become technology, as this would make the experience of a real eudaemonia impossible.

### Be careful what you wish for

The debate over whether we should extend human longevity dramatically—and pursue the end of dying—is a great example of the difficulty of determining whether a particular technological advance will result in human flourishing. It also points toward one of the biggest dilemmas we may be facing soon: If something can be done, does it mean it should be done? Should we consider not doing things because they might also have negative side effects on human flourishing?

Breakthrough gene-editing technologies such as CRISPR-Cas9 may eventually help to end cancer or Alzheimer's, and would clearly contribute to our collective well-being. However, another application of this scientific magic may also bring about programmable babies, dramatically increased longevity, or even the end of dying for humanity—but likely only for those few who have the significant resources that would no doubt be required! How will we make sure the advances will be 95% positive for humanity and not cause social disruption, terrorism, or exponential inequality?

In Silicon Valley, the epicenter of human-technology convergence, Peter Diamandis likes to say, "The question is what would people be willing to spend for an extra 20, 30, 40 years of a healthy life—it's a huge opportunity."[181] That comment speaks volumes about the Silicon Valley philosophy: Everything is a business opportunity—even human happiness!

Consider the rise of what science writer Amy Maxman, writing in *Wired* magazine in July 2015, called "The Genesis Engine," i.e. the concept of editing human DNA.[182] The first step will be the analysis of the DNA of billions of people to identify which genes are responsible for different conditions and diseases. Brute computing power and broad public support for the concept will be required. Second, once a gene has been identified as being responsible for something as detrimental as cancer (assuming it will be that straightforward), the next step will be finding ways to remove or suppress that gene so that the disease does not develop. Third would be the idea of essentially programming people like we program software or apps today—removing all the bad bugs and adding in great features.

Does that strike you as a desirable future? Most people would answer with a resounding "Yes!" because it sounds too good to be true. Yet the mind boggles when we think about what realizing such scientific feats could mean in a broader context: Who could afford such treatments? Who would regulate where they could or could not be applied? Would we open all doors to superhumans, and close the door to plain old humans? Would the possibility of programming our genes mean we would inadvertently be on our way to becoming more like machines?

On the one hand, editing the human genome for the purpose of ending diseases would definitely result in increased well-being and happiness, but the very same capabilities could easily result in civil wars or terrorism. Just imagine if only the super-rich could avoid all life-threatening diseases and live to be 150 years old while everyone else would wither at 90 years old or younger—or not even be able to afford basic healthcare. If there were ever grounds for resorting to civil unrest out of sheer desperation, look no further. How could we even conceive of offering such possibilities without first considering these vexing ethical and societal issues? Why would we spend trillions of euros on STEM, but invest so very little in what I call the CORE humanity issues —creativity and compassion, originality, reciprocity and responsibility, and empathy?

## A positive example

We don't have to look to such extreme examples to find a compelling argument for or against a digitally mediated human experience. Consider Wikipedia, a nonprofit global knowledge base: a positive example of a boost to collective well-being delivered through technology. The creation of Wikipedia, to a very large extent, fueled the betterment of society. At a time when knowledge and information were not readily accessible to all, Wikipedia opened up access to everyone, everywhere—without the costs of paying for old-fashioned dictionaries, libraries, or commercial and government databases.

Admittedly, people around the globe are happy about having Wikipedia, and its co-founder, Jimmy Wales, is widely revered as having furthered the collective progress of society with this innovation. In addition, the unintended consequences of Wikipedia, such as the demise of the printed version of *Encyclopaedia Britannica*, could be viewed as somewhat negligible.

Wikipedia, therefore, makes a good case of technology furthering well-being and human flourishing, but it's certainly not flawless. As a case in point, this author's English-language listing was deleted in 2011 for lack of notability.

In contrast, innovations such as Tinder (a popular dating and messaging app—just in case you have not yet had the pleasure), Google Maps, or the Apple Watch, don't really further collective well-being in the same way as Wikipedia did—even though they are all quite possibly useful and even endearing, they are simply commercial expressions of a "yes we can" approach to lifestyle technology. Useful, yes; furthering general well-being—probably not, or at least not to the same degree as Wikipedia.

### Trading happiness for tech-powered hedonism?

Imagine if we could easily simulate the feeling of intimacy with a human sexual partner by using a good-looking, sophisticated, AI-powered sex robot (yes, this is a rapidly growing industry, in case you were wondering).[183]

By all means, having sex with robots qualifies as a decidedly hedonistic experience. One wonders: Would we still be as interested in pursuing true happiness and a complete sexual experience in an actual, real-life, human-to-human relationship where we actually need to struggle to make it work? Or would we get used to the ease with which sex robots would be available, and therefore just settle for convenience? How tempting would it be to resort to such a consumerist attitude to sex? And, conversely, who are we to deny people the right to enjoy whatever they want?

Sure, you may argue that we would still know the difference, and we certainly would. But how much would we be altered, in our minds, by making constant use of sex robots? Would it not mess with our brains and distort our perception of reality—our views of what the real world is actually like?

Studies of men who routinely watch pornography have shown that extensive use has significant impact on the stimulation required for arousal and for what's required to reach an orgasm.[184] Just imagine how that issue would be magnified by sex robots, which are dead-certain to become very smart, cheap, and incredibly human-like—just watch a few episodes of AMC's *Humans* to see where this could be going.[185]

Does that mean we should ban sex robots because they lead us to inhuman practices? I would propose there would be no harm in banning the next generations of human-like robots, socially and otherwise, but of course that is unlikely to stop their availability. This is but one example of how exponential technological gains (in this case, artificial skin, robotics, and AI) could lead us down the path of hedonistic happiness at an ever faster pace, at lower cost, and with widespread availability.

So the key question is: Will exponential technologies further our well-being, and if so, who would be in charge of making sure that they don't flip, inadvertently or by design? Who decides what is human and what is not, and at what point are we crossing a line that distinguishes us from the tools we have created?

This is the inherent tension between man and machine that technology cannot possibly resolve—even if the entire human brain and its 100 billion neurons could eventually be simulated. Compassion and happiness, like consciousness, simply do not exist in mere biological or chemical terms but in the holistic interplay of everything that is human.

Machines or software are unlikely to ever attain these states, even if they quickly become better at simulating them to some extent. Clearly, computer programs can already measure or detect compassion using facial recognition techniques, and software could probably simulate compassion after having reviewed trillions of variations of facial expressions and linguistic indicators.

Attempts at first defining and then programming a human characteristic such as compassion, or something as mysterious as consciousness, seem like a far-fetched and unrealizable concept in the foreseeable future. But then again, is the real danger that a great simulation will quite possibly be "good enough" for most of us?

I am increasingly worried about the idea that we may sooner or later be okay with having something close enough.

## Putting technology back in its place

I fundamentally believe that computers, software programs, algorithms, and robots are unlikely to ever develop human-like compassion or empathy. Robots and AI as helpers and servants, yes—but certainly never as masters.

Should we really try and utilize mathematical models or machine intelligence to optimize emotional outcomes? And in the context of machine thinking, should we really attempt to deploy better technology to solve social or political problems—such as using overbearing surveillance techniques to end terrorism?

The complex androrithmic values must remain the domain of human beings, both because we are better at creating nuanced expressions of them and because direct engagement with those problems is key to developing eudaemonia—deeper happiness.

I often wonder whether exponential technological progress will generate exponential human happiness, beyond the 1% of those who will create, own, and profit from such brilliant miracle machines. Is it a virtuous goal to construct a perfect human machine that can be freed of all its flaws and inefficiencies, so that we can finally become god, whatever that might mean?

I don't know about you, but that isn't a world I would strive to build. To propose we pursue this path is like gambling with our future and potentially poisoning the well for our children and the generations to come.

Happiness cannot be programmed into machines, automated, or sold. It cannot be copied, codified, or deep-learned. It needs to emanate from and grow within us, and in between us, and technology is here to help us—as a tool. We are a species that uses technology, not a species that is destined to be(come) technology.

Finally, think about this: The word happiness itself stems from a Viking word for luck, *happ*. This also relates to the concept of happenstance, or chance. The apologists for technology may profess that they are removing the negative elements of chance from human lives—which we all know are legion, from disease and poverty, to death itself. However, in doing so, they may be systematically altering the ability of human beings to experience deeper levels of happiness that are not dependent on measurable circumstance. Yes, by all means let us use the tools of technology to remove the dangerous risks of being human on Planet Earth. But no, let's not become the tools of our tools and surrender our mercurial consciousness and sovereign free will for a bunch of trinkets and cheap thrills like the innocent natives of some New World.

# Chapter 10
# Digital Ethics

*Technology has no ethics—but humanity depends on them.*

Let's do some exponential math. If we continue on the current path, in just eight to 12 years—depending on when we start counting—overall technological progress is going to leap from today's pivot point of four to 128. At the same time, the scope of our ethics will continue to limp along on a linear, step-wise, and human scale of improvement, from four to five or six if we're lucky; it will improve just a little bit as we adapt to a new framework.

Even if Moore's Law may eventually cease to apply as far as microchips are concerned, many of the fields of technology, from communications bandwidth to artificial intelligence (AI) and deep learning, are still likely to grow at least exponentially and with combinatorial effects—the changes reinforcing one another.[186]

Zoom forward another ten years, and we may indeed end up 95% automated, hyperconnected, virtualized, uber-efficient, and much less human than we could ever imagine today. A society that sleepwalks down the exponential growth-path of the Megashifts (see chapter 3), a society that does not pause to consider the consequences for human values, beliefs, and ethics, a society that is steered by technologists, venture capitalists, stock markets, and the military, is likely to enter a true machine age.

So what are ethics? Going beyond the simple answer, how one should live, the Greek word *ethos* means custom and habit.[187] Today, we often use ethics as a synonym or as shorthand for morals, values, assumptions, purposes, and beliefs. The primary concern of ethics is to question whether something is right or not in a given circumstance. What feels right to you is governed by your ethics, and in many cases it's hard to explain why something does not feel right. That is clearly one of the challenges of agreeing on even the most basic ethical rules for the exponential age we are about to enter. Nevertheless, later on I shall attempt to formulate some ethical rules—or principles to guide technology development.

> *"Today the needful work is to distinguish ourselves from our machines. It's to rediscover, for example, that all knowledge is knowledge of man, and that nothing worth calling an ideal can be found in an engineered world, but only in ourselves." –Stephen Talbott*[188]

The bio-ethicist Larry Churchill suggests, "Ethics, understood as the capacity to think critically about moral values and direct our actions in terms of such values, is a generic human capacity."[189]

So if ethics—to think critically about moral values and direct our actions accordingly—is indeed a generic human capacity, should we (a) never expect machines or computers to really understand them, and therefore be very cautious about their increasing self-learning capacities, or (b) try to encode some kind of basic ethics into software and teach our machines to at least understand and respect them—the topic of so-called machine ethics?[190] This is an important question we will seek to answer here.

### What happens to our ethics if machines become self-learning?

Ethical questions arise quickly alongside the exponential progress of technology, for example, with self-driving cars, whom should the car run over if an accident is totally unavoidable? In the case of home-care robots, what should the robot do if the patient refuses to take her medication? When machines stop following pre-programmed decision trees and start learning things themselves, will they also learn those things that even humans find hard to express and codify?

Humans don't simply hard-code decisions such as "If this patient has a 35% chance of a life-threatening medical issue, then she must take these medications even if force is required." Of course, humans do different things at different times, and they do make mistakes. Would we accept that from a robot, and would we accept being treated in such a way by a robot?

In his 1942 short story *Runaround*, science fiction writer Isaac Asimov defined the now infamous Three Laws of Robotics:

1. A robot may not injure a human being or, through inaction, allow a human being to come to harm.
2. A robot must obey the orders given it by human beings except where such orders would conflict with the First Law.
3. A robot must protect its own existence as long as such protection does not conflict with the First or Second Laws.

Are these laws still pertinent, today, and would they go straight out of the window with machines that self-learn? Maybe a care robot would need to harm human beings (albeit marginally) because another, more authorized human being (for example, a doctor) commanded it to enforce medication. How would our robot know where to start and where to stop? Would our software lock the refrigerator if we're on a strict diet? Would it turn off the phone and Internet to prevent us from ordering a pizza? Monitor our toilet for signs of unplanned consumption?

In this context it's quite clear that no AI will ever be truly intelligent without some kind of ethical governance module because without it, the AI would likely miss the last few ethical pieces of the puzzle that humans would consider, and would therefore always fail when it matters most. Imagine an AI that drives your autonomous vehicle not knowing when it is and when it isn't OK to kill an animal that's on the road.

Yet even if we were to make robots intelligent in terms of learning and self-derived decision making, today they are still close to point zero in terms of emotional and social intelligence—two terms that are in themselves very hard to explain or even measure.

The issue of learning machines is one of my chief concerns when it comes to ethics. Deep learning is the area of AI that has seen the biggest investments since 2015[191] and this is very likely to continue in the next few years. We are not going to see another AI winter, another period where investors will stop funding AI ventures because they over-promised and under-delivered.

Just imagine if (when?) infinitely powerful machines and supercomputers are able to learn how to solve pretty much any problem based only on a huge flow of live data, i.e. without any prior commands or programming. Google DeepMind's AlphaGo victory, discussed earlier, is a prime example of such learning capabilities in action.[192]

With deep learning, powerful machines can discover the underlying soft rules, values, and principles, and could therefore understand and quite possibly even simulate them. However, if this is destined to become the next big thing in computing (as IBM likes to say, "cognitive computing"), we mere humans would have no way to gauge if the AI's recommendations are correct or not, because the machines' computational capabilities would dramatically exceed our own. A wicked problem indeed, if we invent machines that are several orders of magnitude beyond our own capabilities, with IQs of 50,000 and above, how do we know they can be trusted? And who can still supervise them? Would they eventually become sentient in some new way? Should we embed a set of desirable human ethics in them, and how would that even be possible?

In his 1987 *AI* magazine article "A Question of Responsibility," Mitchell Waldrop wrote:

One thing that is apparent . . . is that intelligent machines will embody values, assumptions, and purposes, whether their programmers consciously intend them to or not. Thus, as computers and robots become more and more intelligent, it becomes imperative that we think carefully and explicitly about what those built-in values are.[193]

This issue has even more relevance as we enter the exponential era because we must now consider what the ethical frameworks should be for all exponential technologies including AI, geo-engineering, cognitive computing, and of course, human genome editing in particular. This includes both the frameworks that are (in)advertently programmed into machines by their human inventors or builders, as well as those that machines may themselves learn and evolve over time.

If IBM's Watson is a true thinking machine, how will it deal with human parameters and values that are unclear, ambiguous, or unspoken even between humans? Will these AI ethics be hard-wired through pre-programming or evolved and adapted using deep learning neural networks that seek to mimic how the brain acquires new information? And if they are self-learning, how will humans be able to verify, control, and adjust them? How would these systems cater to the myriad cultural permutations of human ethics?

The deeper scientific questions about AI and deep learning, such as the technical feasibility of controlling such new intelligences, are beyond the scope of this author and this book, for now, but in any case, it's obvious that a humongous task lies ahead of us. Indeed, in the very near future, the role of a digital ethicist may well become one of the most sought-after jobs along with data scientist. Maybe this is a good job for your kids, as well . . . ?

### And no religion, too. . .?

It is also very important to remind ourselves that ethics are not at all the same as religion. In his enlightening 2011 book *Beyond Religion*, the Dalai Lama remarked that everybody has ethics and only some people have religion, and then called for the establishment of global secular ethics to guide our most elemental decisions such as those on autonomous weapons systems with the power to kill without human supervision.[194] Ethics versus religion is an essential distinction we need to maintain when discussing hot-button topics such a human genome editing or nonbiological augmentations of humans. I suggest that we should avoid bringing religion into these debates as much as we can because religious views are not nearly as uniform and ubiquitous as the most basic ethics and values, and because they are front-loaded with too much history and past experiences.

Arthur C. Clarke highlighted this critical distinction in a 1999 interview:

> So now people assume that religion and morality have a necessary connection. But the basis of morality is really very simple and doesn't require religion at all.[195]

### Creating a Global Digital Ethics Council: How would we define ethics that are fit for the exponential age?

I would like to address two main concerns: Firstly, to try and define what a globally agreeable set of ethics could be for an exponentially Digital Age; and secondly, to try and define what we would need to do to ensure that human well-being and ethical concerns actually remain on top of the agenda globally, and are not taken over by machine thinking.

We need to define a set of bottom-line digital ethics—ethics that are fit for the Digital Age: open enough not to put the brakes on progress or hamper innovation, yet strong enough to protect our humanness. A compass, not a map, towards a future that will see increasingly powerful technologies first empower, then augment and then increasingly threaten humanity.

To this end, I propose that we create a Global Digital Ethics Council (GDEC) tasked with defining what the ground rules and most basic and universal values of such a dramatically different, fully digitized society should be.

By and large at present we agree that no rogue states should have nuclear capabilities even if they can afford them. This situation is indeed complex, fraught with lies and deception—and always changing—but the essential understanding remains, and is enforced because the alternative involves untold risk.

In the same way, we now need to agree on the limits and independent monitoring of both the scope and progress in future AI, genome editing, and other exponential technologies.

To kick-start this conversation, I have set out some straw man suggestions below. I know this is a daunting task, and yes, sure, it may even be presumptuous to try. But we need to get started, so I might as well get burned first!

To support the GDEC, we also need to set out a simple manifesto on digital ethics, a kind of global treaty on exponential human rights in an increasingly digital world. Such a manifesto and subsequent treaty could serve to guide and hold accountable those companies that invent, make, and sell these technologies (and their governments). This is really important because the implications of exponential technological change on human existence can no longer be treated as mere externalities, as a side effect that is of no immediate concern to those causing it.

The GDEC I envision would need to include well-informed and deep-thinking individuals from civil society, academia, government, business, and technology, as well as independent thinkers, writers, artists, and thought leaders. (This writer is happy to chime in!) It needs to be global from the outset, and might eventually need similar or even larger powers to those which UN Human Rights Special Rapporteurs have today—namely the right to monitor, advise, and publicly report issues and violations.[196]

As used to be the case with sustainability, ethics are often a final, "nice to have" item on the agenda that can be bumped whenever something more urgent comes up. This is a fundamentally flawed and very dangerous approach to safeguarding our futures. As we move into an era where critical developments will happen gradually then suddenly, we simply won't have the runway to consider our ethics at the point when they have already been irretrievably squashed by thinking machines. "Wait and See" simply means human abdication.

## A new moral calculus

We must spend as much time and resources on digital ethics as we spend on exponential technologies. Examining the unintended consequences of exponential technologies and preventing damage to humanity—going far beyond the existential risks—demands as much support as we are giving to the sciences now driving those changes. The human factor requires just as much funding and promotion as science—there can be no STEM (science, technology, engineering and mathematics) without its CORE (creativity, originality, reciprocity and empathy).

In his 2015 book *Machines of Loving Grace*, *New York Times* reporter John Markoff highlights the need for this new moral calculus:

> Optimists hope that the potential abuses of our computer systems will be minimized if the application of artificial intelligence, genetic engineering, and robotics remains focused on humans rather than algorithms. But the tech industry has not had a track record that speaks to moral enlightenment. It would be truly remarkable if a Silicon Valley company rejected a profitable technology for ethical reasons. Today, decisions about implementing technology are made largely on the basis of profitability and efficiency. What is needed is a new moral calculus.[197]

## Five new human rights for the Digital Age

Here are five core human rights that I humbly suggest might form part of a future Digital Ethics Manifesto:

1. **The right to remain natural, i.e. biological** – We must have the choice to exist in an unaugmented state. We need to retain the right to be employed, use public services, buy things, and function in society without the need to deploy technology on or inside our bodies. These #WiredOrFired fears are already an

issue (albeit deemed mostly harmless) as far as mobile devices and social media are concerned. However, one can easily imagine a future where we may be forced to wear augmented reality (AR)/virtual reality (VR) glasses, visors, or helmets to qualify for employment, or even worse, be required to use or implant specific wetware apps as a condition of employment. Mere humans would no longer be good enough—and this isn't a desirable future.

2. **The right to be inefficient if and where it defines our basic humanness** – We must have the choice to be slower than technology. We should not make efficiency more important than humanity. It may soon be vastly more efficient and much cheaper to use digital health diagnostics via platforms like Scanadu than to see a doctor every time I have a medical issue. I believe these technologies are in the main positive and could be one of the keys to lowering the cost of healthcare. However, does this mean we should penalize people who choose to do otherwise, or force compliance upon those that don't want their health data in the cloud?

3. **The right to disconnect** – We must retain the right to switch off connectivity, to "go dark" on the network, and to pause communications, tracking, and monitoring. We can expect many employers and companies to make hyperconnectivity a default requirement in the near future. As an employee or insured driver you may become liable for unauthorized disconnection if you and/or your car can no longer be tracked on the network.

   To be self-contained and technically disconnected at times of our own choosing is a fundamentally important right because disconnecting allows us to refocus on our unmediated environment and to be in the moment. It also reduces the risk of digital obesity (see chapter 7) and lessens the reach of inadvertent surveillance. Offline may be the new luxury, but it should remain a basic right.

4. **The right to be anonymous** – In this coming hyperconnected

world, we should still have the option of not being identified and tracked, such as when using a digital application or platform, or when commenting or criticizing if it's harmless to others and does not infringe on anyone else. Sure, there are some obvious occasions where real anonymity would be impossible and probably unreasonable to expect, such as in digital banking transactions. However, we should make sure that protected spaces remain, where complete tracking isn't required or the norm, such as when voicing political opinions, sharing personal pictures, or getting medical advice. Anonymity, mystery, serendipity, and mistakes are crucial human attributes we should not seek to remove by technological means.

5. **The right to employ or involve people instead of machines** – We should not allow companies or employers to be disadvantaged if they choose to use people instead of machines, even if it's more expensive and less efficient. Instead we should provide tax credits to those that do, and consider automation taxes for companies that dramatically reduce the number of employees in favor of machines and software. Those taxes would need to be made available to retrain people that became the victims of technological unemployment.

It's important to note that many of these rights touch on an important issue at the core of this debate: How much freedom are we willing to sacrifice in order to be either more efficient or more secure? We also need to ask what the ethics of security should be, and how will technology deal with this crucial issue?

## 15 daring Shall Not's
In furtherance of developing and embedding clear and globally consistent digital ethics, here are some specific examples of technological pitfalls that we should avoid if we want humanity to prevail.

I am keenly aware that, in providing thought starters for the debate, some of these suggested commandments might turn out to be overly simplified, idealistic, impractical, utopian, incomplete, and controversial. Hence, I am humbly presenting them simply in the spirit of starting a discussion.

1.  We shall not require or plan for humans to gradually become technology themselves, just because that would satisfy technology or technology companies and/or stimulate growth.
2.  We shall not allow humans to be governed or essentially directed by technologies such as AI, the IoT and robotics.
3.  We shall not alter human nature by programming or manufacturing new creatures with the help of technology.
4.  We shall not augment humans in order to achieve supernatural powers that would eliminate the clear distinction between man and machine.
5.  We shall not empower machines to empower themselves, and thereby circumvent human control.
6.  We shall not seek to replace trust with tracking in our communications and relationships just because technology makes this universally possible.
7.  We shall not plan for, justify, or desire total surveillance because of a perceived need for total security.
8.  We shall not allow bots, machines, platforms, or other intelligent technologies to take over essential democratic functions in our society which should actually be carried out by humans themselves.
9.  We shall not seek to diminish or replace real-life human culture with algorithmic, augmented, or virtual simulations.
10. We shall not seek to minimize human flaws just to make a better fit with technology.
11. We shall not attempt to abolish mistakes, mystery, accidents, and chance by using technology to predict or prevent them, and we shall not strive to make everything explicit just because technology may make it feasible to do so.
12. We shall not create, engineer, or distribute any technology

with the primary goal of generating addiction to it.

13. We shall not require robots to make moral decisions, or equip them to challenge our decisions.

14. We shall not demand or stipulate that humans should also be exponential in nature.

15. We shall not confuse a clean algorithm for an accurate picture of human reality ("software is cheating the world"), and we shall not give undue power to technology because it generates economic benefits.

On the particular issue of everything becoming explicit, social networks are teaching us a good lesson: Things that used to be unspoken—living between the lines—have subtly become the focus of attention, announced very clearly, and amplified by groupthink. While my endorsement of a given civil rights group, a political organization, or a social cause may have been explicit in the past, the information was not widely available to everyone. Now that everything is connected, my every comment can be seen instantly, examined, and aggregated by everyone.

## We must not pursue efficiency over humanity

Exponential technologies are quickly making everything around us increasingly more efficient. As a result, everything is becoming a service, everything is in the cloud, and everything is now smart. Even the dumbest piece of hardware will have sensors, contributing to a global tsunami of data that, paired with AI, may hold the solution to pretty much any problem.[198]

Let's imagine what such a world could look like by 2030. When literally everything is tracked, measured, and hyper-efficient, what will happen to things that cannot be quantified as easily? What will we do about emotions, surprise, hesitation, uncertainty, contemplation, mystery, mistakes, accidents, serendipity, and other distinct human traits? Would they become undesirable because algorithms and machines are perfect, programmed not to make mistakes, work 24/7/365, don't have unions, and by and large will do as they are told?

(Well, at least the non-thinking kind will…).

Will increasing technological progress mean that humans who exhibit too many of these non-machine-readable traits will be considered a waste of time, or worse, be treated like sand in the gearbox of big efficiency?

Will we increasingly adapt and change our behavior, so we can appear to be more efficient, or at least pretend to be? Will the idea of total efficiency become the great equalizer forcing us to behave more uniformly? Will the obsession with technology and its absolute efficiency and consistency eventually overrule the tacit acceptance of human inefficiency and difference? This often seems likely to me, even if it may take longer here in Europe—and even longer than that here in Switzerland!

If reaching the highest possible efficiency will remain a primary concern, then skyrocketing machine performance in the exponential age means we would probably not have any human involvement in anything at all, before long. Moving from four to 128 on the technology scale in the next decade or so suggests that many tasks could be 32 times faster than today. Can you imagine retail, banking, and transportation becoming 32 times as efficient as today? Would they be 32 times cheaper as well, and if so, what would that mean for our economy?

We will need to be very careful when making decisions based purely on efficiency that will almost certainly cost human jobs, remove human authority, or otherwise cause humans to automate, assignate, and abdicate (see chapter 4).

In many cases we may need to live with those dreaded inefficiencies, and accept that they are simply a part of human life, even if they create obstacles to automation. The alternative would be to enforce efficiency ruthlessly, and do away with those who don't comply: If you want to see your doctor in person rather than use the remote diagnosis device, you will pay a penalty. Not having your car tracked at all times will mean you'll lose your insurance coverage. Not accepting a chip implant means you cannot work in this company.

The medical sector offers some useful precedents here for the debates that are yet to come. Some people have long argued that caesarians are more efficient than natural childbirths, and therefore we should forego that privilege altogether—a clear case of putting efficiency over humanity.[199] Witnessing the exponential power of technology, I have a hunch where this might be going next: exogenesis—pregnancy outside the womb, babies born in labs.

Would it be efficient to track your car or any other means of transportation 100% of the time, on every parameter such as speed, direction, acceleration, interior temperature, and exterior air quality? The answer is yes. But would it also serve a human-worthy purpose? In many ways the answer is also yes: Using autonomous vehicles and analyzing tracking data could help to reduce pollution significantly, and put an end to most accidents. But in many other ways, constant tracking would be detrimental as well because it would be the most perfect surveillance tool ever invented, and would force us to act in a compliant manner at all times.

We urgently need to ask ourselves if we really want to replace our innate human sensibilities and capabilities with the promise of perfect machine functionalities, and gradually chisel away at the very meaning of being human. We may end up making things ultra-efficient, but we would be robbing ourselves of all purpose.

What if only the wealthiest 2% get access to new genetic treatments that promise dramatic life extension and longevity, while everyone else is locked out? Would we see even more civil unrest and terrorism due to even deeper inequality—driven by exponential technological gains? Just imagine what would happen if such a "DNA-fix" for aging emerges, but only millionaires could afford the treatment to live to 150, while everyone else died more or less as usual. It seems clear that our current ethical paradigms, under pressure from business-as-usual capitalism and stock market expectations, have no answer for these dilemmas.

## Life beyond the algorithm
So what can we do about technology taking over where it should not? How can we protect ourselves from merely becoming the objects of

bot-fueled hyper-efficiency, feeding a giant AI that in turn dictates our lives and tells us what we can no longer do?

We need to ask if we're doing something because it's inefficient for machines or because it's positive for human users, and we need to ask this question a lot more often. We need to ask this question when voting for new laws, when starting a business, and when we give our money to technology companies. Voting with our wallets is a powerful tool that consumers have not used enough where digital ethics are concerned. Ironically, with technology, that right will become ever easier to exercise.

The ethical question, the issue of purpose and meaning, must come before the question of feasibility and cost. Going forward, the primary question in technology won't be about if something can be done, but why, when, where and by whom it should be done.

Another response may just be to say no, to refuse participation more often, to reject technologies and processes, apps, and software that are clearly not fit for human use but would simply amplify the power of algorithms. Maybe we should devise a health warning sticker or stamp like we have on cigarette boxes today, telling us that this program, app, or device "is certain not to further human happiness."

While efficiency and increased profit is sometimes a worthwhile goal, and ultimately one of the cornerstones of capitalism, we should not use technology to further a shortcut/wormhole-belief that purports efficiency alone to be the most important and worthy and human goal. This is machine thinking that won't serve us in the long term.

# Chapter 11
# Earth 2030: Heaven or Hell?

*While many of the seismic changes on the horizon are to be welcomed—like working for a passion rather than for a living—several of the most basic privileges we once took for granted—like freedom of choice in consumption and independent free will in lifestyle—could become vestigial echoes or the preserves of ultra high-net-worth individuals. Heaven or Hell?*

As I write this in 2016, we are already at the point where much of what used to be considered science fiction is already becoming science fact.

We are already experiencing the science fiction and, sometimes, the adverse effects of the choices of previous generations: automated language translation, nearly autonomous cars, nanobots in your bloodstream, artificial intelligence (AI) that can wage cyber wars on our behalf, and refrigerators that talk to our smartphones—which in turn send our data to our doctors.

So, let's zoom forward to 2030, visualize plausible futures for a world reshaped by exponential technological change, and consider what some HellVen (#hellven) scenarios may look like. Presented below is a timeline of possible scenarios stretching out to 2030.

## 2020: Hyperconnectivity and hyper-manipulation
As everything is now hyperconnecting, all ten major global brains—formerly Internet platforms and media companies—use algorithms to measure and determine what I should see, when, and how.

Back in 2016, a mutually loved little company called Facebook was using algorithms to generate perfect news matches with my profile, ensuring that I stayed engaged with its platform as long as possible, preventing too many dissenting views or negative messages from getting through to me.

Today, as six billion people are "always on" across the planet, all of us see different information and content all the time. We interact with these platforms via augmented reality (AR), virtual reality (VR), and holographic screens, or via intelligent digital assistants (IDA) and bots, old-fashioned apps, and what used to be called websites. In 2020, traditional websites are fading as fast as gasoline-powered cars because AIs in the cloud are now doing the work for us instead—and they don't need eye-catching graphical interfaces or clever designs.

Human editors are signing off too, as big data, smart clouds, and AI have proven to be much more efficient, popular, and virtually free. Plus, they don't object to anything—and advertisers, brands, and political parties can better leverage these systems and spend their marketing budgets more efficiently.

Prediction algorithms are helping to prevent crime. Using publicly available data feeds from police, traffic, public works, welfare, and planning departments, cities can pinpoint trouble spots. They can then cross-reference this information with data extracted from social media feeds, emails, wireless activity, and much more. AI analyzes the data, discovers new correlations, and suggests measures that may prevent crimes, such as increased police patrols, isolating repeat offenders, or alerting potential perpetrators that they are being watched.

**In 2020, the world is becoming hyperconnected, automated, and uber-smart—and everyone benefits.**

### 2022: My best friend is in the cloud

Swarms of IDAs and software bots live in the cloud, taking care of many routine tasks.

- No more searching for the best restaurants or hotels—our travel bots have already done it for us.
- No more updating our doctor on what's wrong—our health bots have already briefed her, or more likely, her bot.
- No more figuring out how to get from one place to another— the transport bots have arranged everything for us already.
- No more searching for anything—our bots know us and our desires and communicate them infinitely better than anything we can express by typing questions into a computer. Literally every search has already been anticipated and the answers are ready for us when we need them.

My digital ego in the cloud has become a true copy of myself thanks to a combination of fast, cheap, and ultra-powerful tools, including mobile cloud technologies, personalization, voice and image recognition, mood analytics, and sentiment analysis. It does not as yet have a body, but it does read my body's data—all the time. It does not have true feelings, but it certainly reads mine. This digital copy of myself has become known as HelloMe.

HelloMe listens, observes, syncs, and simulates me, and as far as my data is concerned, it knows me far better than any human ever would. My digital ego is connected to other bots and AIs that have become very good companions. If I need information, recommendations, and conversations, I or my IDA ask the cloud; if I get lonely, I call upon HelloMe to talk to me, just as I would with a friend—but without all the history, commitments, and coordination hassle. Mobile devices have become integrated onto and into my body, using AR/VR overlays on my glasses, visors, or contact lenses, and very soon we will enjoy neural implants to get rid of any external interface whatsoever.

What Hello Barbie was for young children in 2015, HelloMe is for us today—a smart, friendly, and ubiquitous voice in the sky that really understands me, and that makes my life so much easier.

Over time, I have built a relationship with HelloMe, and I now consider it a dear friend. I cannot wait until HelloMe can reproduce other people's egos that may no longer be available—for example, if they have died or removed themselves from connecting with me as happened with my ex-lover. Soon, HelloMe will be able to communicate exactly like that person—anytime, anywhere—making tedious and time-consuming relationship-building a thing of the past.

We have also added a robotic body to the equation. . . Paralyzed people can now control external exoskeletons so they can walk again, and the costs are dropping dramatically. Brain-computer interfaces (BCI) are being used to pilot aircraft and giant container ships. Turning our thoughts and associated brain activity into triggers for computers is changing how we interact with machines in all segments of business and culture. We are freer than ever to contemplate, create, question, and ponder.

Rather than taking medication to reduce the worst effects of a condition such as high cholesterol, high blood pressure, or diabetes, we are becoming ever better at identifying what causes the disease in the first place. We are starting to employ nanotechnology, AI, and cloud biology to tackle our core health issues. We have identified the genes that may control the advent of certain cancers. Once we know how to manipulate those genes safely, we will be on our way to engineering our way around those diseases. Heaven or hell?

**In 2022, my digital ego has moved to the cloud and is developing a life of its own.**

### 2024: Goodbye privacy and anonymity

Technology has become so fast, powerful, and pervasive that we cannot avoid being tracked, observed, recorded, and monitored—ever. The Internet of Things (IoT) has connected our cars, houses, appliances, parks and cities, consumer goods, medications, drugs, and of course our gadgets and machines. The Internet of Everything connects our minds to the network. The once totally futuristic concept of a second neocortex—a direct connection to an external brain in the cloud—is slowly becoming reality. The hottest new turf for start-ups is in developing and providing add-ons and backup services for machine-based neural networks that will eventually connect directly to our own neocortex via BCIs.

Mobile devices are now almost entirely voice- and gesture-controlled. Most computers have become invisible—always there, always watching, always listening, and always at our command.

Connectivity is ubiquitous: 90% of the world is connected at very high speed and very low cost. Nothing and no one is offline, ever—unless you can afford the luxury of disconnecting or visit one of the offline worlds, such as the Swiss Alps, that have become popular "digital detox" vacation destinations. Offline is the new luxury, no doubt.

Disconnection or refusal to share personal data is socially unacceptable and economically penalized. The penalties can include a dramatic reduction of access to essential services such as navigation, transport, and mobility, as well as steep premiums for services such as insurance and healthcare: If you don't give your data, you don't get the service. Real pre-Internet-era style privacy is only for the very very rich because only they can afford to use technology that orchestrates their digital lives and pays for the benefits without suffering the panopticon effect (all that happens will be watched). Digital surrogates—embodied bots that represent real people—are all the rage but extremely expensive, and their status and legality are often unclear.

You're either wired or fired. Since everything around us is connected, tracked, and monitored, it has become mandatory to be completely wired while at work. And "at work" no longer means being at a certain desk in a certain building. Many people who have questioned this kind of work environment are now out of a job because they lagged behind in productivity ratings—which are, of course, overseen by a bot!

Employers find the increased efficiency irresistible. AR, virtual devices, and apps now make it easy to zoom through large amounts of data or media. An array of tools can provide deep multi-sensory immersion in complex topics that used to take dozens of people and many days of work. It's like our brain is connected to a second neocortex in the cloud, allowing us to go into an entirely new neural performance space that transcends our previous limitations.

There are no secrets left. All we need do is speak to a machine, anytime, anywhere, and it will find the answers for us—mostly for free, yet some information will only be available for a very steep fee. The prediction and profiling business is exploding, making 2016's data mining outfits look Stone Age by comparison. Face scanning technology is so advanced that it can read thousands of faces in split seconds, archive emotional expressions, and create complete face maps of what we were feeling, anywhere, anytime.

The global brains built by the 14 leading big tech companies and platforms are gathering data on six billion connected users all the time, everywhere. Enormously powerful AI assembles our profiles, then deduces who we are, and what we may be doing next. This is a gold mine for security services, police, and governments, and it turbocharges marketing, advertising, and business in general.

Money has gone completely digital, removing the last refuge of anonymity. Paying with cash is the past and mostly forbidden. Every breath mint, latte macchiato, bus ticket, or extra shot of whiskey is on the books (or rather, in the cloud), recorded somewhere, shared somewhere, raising flags somewhere, and contributing to what the global brains know about you. Digital money has also made it impossible to receive cash from anyone—no more moonlighting, no more tax-free tips, no more white lies on your tax return.

The banks are losing huge income streams that used to come from their outrageous money-transfer charges, processing fees, and clueless investment advice—but now they also get to be in the data and platform business. Now, there is a lot more to sell than just financial services; consumers' data has become the new currency of financial institutions. Data isn't just the new oil—now it's also the new money.

Crime and wars are mostly digital. Now that everything and everyone is connected and everything is a real-time data source, we have become completely dependent on connectivity. Anything that disrupts it is considered an assault on "the system." Attacks on technology infrastructure, unauthorized access to our data, and information manipulation have become a constant threat, and over 50% of each nation's military budget is being used to fight security breaches, cybercrime, and digital battles of all kinds. The battleground is digital, and AIs are the new soldiers.

Soon, even thinking will no longer be a private act. Cheap and easy-to-use BCIs and implants are starting to show up everywhere, allowing some communication directly to and from our brains, extending our neocortex into the cloud. Every thought causes a physical reaction in our brains and bodies, which very soon can be recorded and at least partially used for personal health, entertainment, and security.

**In 2024, we are constantly connected to machines, and they are getting better and better at reading our minds.**

### 2026: The automation of everything and the basic income guarantee

Gone are the days when routine tasks—whether blue collar, white collar, manual, or cognitive—were done by a human. Machines have learned how to understand language, images, emotions, and beliefs. Machines can also speak, write, draw, and simulate human emotions. Machines cannot be, but they can think. Hundreds of millions of jobs are being handed over to machines in call centers, maintenance, accounting, legal, retail, manufacturing, and financial services. Research and development is now done by machines as well. We saw the first examples of AIs working as scientists some ten years ago. By 2020 they were starting to beat human scientists in the speed of scientific discovery. Robots now routinely digest billions of data feeds and run experiments in the cloud, yielding completely new approaches to fundamental scientific challenges.

Human-only jobs are becoming rarer and rarer, but in general, anything that cannot be digitized, automated, virtualized, or robotized is becoming more valuable all the time. Pairing people with machines is the new normal—in most situations, a machine working with a human still beats any machine without human involvement.

Income is starting to decouple from work, and remuneration

is detaching from the number of hours worked. Being paid for results, outcomes, and performance is emerging as the dominant remuneration model. Working less is finally the new normal (surely heaven to many).

Costs for most consumer goods and services such as transportation, housing, media, and communications are falling dramatically because machines are doing all the heavy lifting and are making most products and services so much cheaper. The only thing that keeps getting more expensive is choosing not to be tracked and monitored all the time.

The economic logic of working for a living is evaporating; instead, we are starting to work for a purpose. A basic income guarantee (BIG) is already in place in 12 countries including Switzerland and Finland, and it's widely expected to become a global standard in the next two decades, ringing in a new post-capitalist era.

With machines doing all the hard work, increasing numbers of people are doing what they want to do rather than what pays the bills. The BIG has become a key factor in societal happiness, fueling a new boom in arts and crafts, entrepreneurship, and public intellectualism.

**In 2026, automation is widespread, jobs are in decline, and social norms are being rewritten.**

### 2028: Free will is only for the rich

Because everything we do, say, see and, increasingly, feel and think, can be tracked and measured, we have seen a waning in the importance of free will, our ancestral ability to make our own decisions without external pressures forcing us into compliance. We can no longer easily divert from what the system thinks is best for us, because everything is observed. This makes for healthier and more responsible lives, lowers the costs of medical care, and makes near-perfect security possible. Yet, many of us are not sure if this is heaven or hell.

We no longer control our own diet because obesity and over-consumption have proven to be major burdens on public health systems worldwide. Sugar, tobacco, alcohol, and caffeine are strictly controlled substances. Everyone must routinely submit to monitoring procedures, both on the incoming side (food) as well as on the outgoing end (human waste).

3D printers long ago became as cheap as inkjet printers, with the biggest cost being the ink and the ingredients that feed the printer. Food printers now use organic and wholesome components to print pizzas, cakes, bread, and desserts on demand, and much more is possible using artificial components. Food is becoming as abundant as information, music, and video.

However, our shopping list is determined by what we are allowed to consume, which is determined by our data feed into the health cloud. Refrigerators won't unlock their food compartments until a predetermined time, and restaurants won't serve us food that isn't cleared with our IDA.

In the end, this is so much better for everyone: People are healthier, governments are saving money, and the fast-moving consumer goods companies now have a direct way to market a 100% personalized product to every single consumer.

Unless, of course, you have unlimited resources to rig the system, buy or create fake digital identities, gain access to one of those really expensive 3D food printers, or source food from dark-net markets such as the Milk Road—a successor to the Silk Road black market site of the early 21st century.

But, as we now know, free will has always been overrated!

**In 2028, our lives have become tracked, guided, and curated; free will and free choice are the preserve of the super-rich.**

### 2030: 90 is the new 60
By 2030, technology and pharma have converged almost completely. Mankind's biggest diseases, including cancer, diabetes, heart disease, and AIDS are being tackled by advanced bioengineering. Nowadays, we very rarely take pills to fight sickness or diseases; instead, we increasingly use technology and genetic editing to observe, predict,

and prevent the onset of diseases.

Because we have analyzed the DNA of billions of connected humans via cloud biology and quantum computing, we can now determine with great certainty which exact gene is responsible for triggering which exact disease. In another five years or so we will be able to prevent cancer.

Longevity has exploded, completely changing our social systems as well. Since most of us can live very healthily until we're 90, and since robots and software are doing most of the hard work for us, we can spend our time helping the next generations understand the past and discover the future. Because BIG has been instituted in many cities and nations, we don't have to worry about retirement or earning a living like our fathers and mothers did.

**In 2030, society is older, healthier, liberated from work, and pursuing meaning.**

### HellVen—an inevitable path?

The future—what's not to like? The scenarios are plausible and—if anything—a little conservative compared to the techno-progressive visions and aspirations. Technology has won the war with humanity, which may not have been a war at all. What need is there for old-fashioned human values and serendipity when the risks and downsides of being alive are being eradicated at such breakneck speed?

**With mankind finally in control of its own future, who needs another future to dream of?**

# Chapter 12
# Decision Time

*It's time to choose your team.*

This book was inspired by the work of so many people that have expressed similar concerns, and I can only hope it will help shape a global debate on the purpose and ethics of technology—and the ethics of those who invent and provide it.

Humans and technology are increasingly overlapping, intersecting, or even converging—your choice of words depends very much on how you feel about that fact. In any case, as stated at the very beginning of this book, this much is certain: I believe humanity is likely to change more in the next 20 years than the previous 300 years.

The coming man-machine confluence will enable amazing wins for humanity and simultaneously threaten it. We must now become much better stewards of our inventions and their consequences if we are to flourish.

Yes, technological progress seems unstoppable because it's the nature of humans to conjure, test, and deploy our *techne* (our tools). Yet finally, we have reached the point where human-centric policies and standards, digital ethics, social contracts, and global agreements on humanizing these exponential technologies will be as important as nuclear nonproliferation treaties.

In the very near future, it will no longer be about whether technology can do something (the answer will almost always be yes) but whether it should do something—and why.

The danger is that if we don't spend as much time and resources on the androrithms (those qualities that make us human) as we do on the algorithms, not only will technology end up running our lives, but we will also be forced, tricked, or otherwise cajoled into becoming technology ourselves. We shall have become "the tools of our tools."

Note that by "technology running our lives," I don't mean the robot overlords of *Terminator Genisys*.[200] Rather, I am concerned that we may soon become completely useless without technology—slow, incomplete, dumb, deskilled, lazy, and obese.

Imagine what would happen if we continued to chip away at and ultimately erode quintessential human qualities such as privacy, mystery, anonymity, emotions, spontaneity, surprise, intuition, imagination, and spirituality—just so that we can keep up with the machines.

If we don't want to become technology ourselves; if we don't want to be increasingly assimilated into the powerful vortex created by the Megashifts; if we want to remain "naturally human" in spite of the powerful lures of those magical technologies; if we want to safeguard what truly makes us happy and not just what makes us function, we must take action while we still have the wiggle room. That time is now.

We must start asking why, followed by who, and when, not just if and how. We must ask questions about purpose, not just about profits. We must increasingly question industry leaders and especially technologists and the firms that employ them. We must compel them all to take a more holistic view, to consider the good as well as the not-so-good implications of what they are proposing. We must also ask them to acknowledge and address those unintended consequences, and to include the externalities of whatever they are creating in their business plans and revenue models.

We must hold the creators and financiers of tomorrow—and of course ourselves, as users and consumers—responsible at every turn. We need to start denying customership to those companies that don't care enough, and we must stop being the content for those platforms that are seeking to automate us. We must stop being silent contributors to machine thinking because everything else is less convenient.

If we don't want to end up with what I call the Oppenheimer Regret—named after the famous physicist J. Robert Oppenheimer, whose inventions made the atomic bomb a reality, and who subsequently regretted his actions and their consequences—we must commit to being on "team human," to put humanity first and above all.

Therefore, I propose that we try and define some basic ground rules for this coming machine age by determining which technologies, if applied, will most likely promote human flourishing and should therefore be pursued, and which technologies will not. We must also ask the "when, why, and who" questions more often, and we also need to think about who would actually control compliance with those rules.

This will be a huge task, to be sure, and certainly fraught with uncertainty about whether we can agree on even the most basic rules for humanity.

Nevertheless, if we want to master those imminent clashes between humans and machines described in this book, we will need a new kind of global stewardship backed up by ever more prescient foresights. We will need the ground rules to be decisive yet flexible enough not to inhibit progress. Daunting? Yes. Impossible? No. Alternatives? None.

**Nine suggested principles**
To help fuel the debate on the best way forward, I have framed nine principles. They capture the essence of the core arguments I've presented through the pages of this book, but they are still a work in progress and far from complete or conclusive.

1. **We need to become much better at understanding exponentiality and what it means for the future of humanity.** We must learn how to imagine and then live with exponential and combinatorial changes. In our immediate future, "wait and see" is just as bad as "just do it." "Gradually, then suddenly" is indeed the new normal and we should not waste our runways

into the future while we still have them in front of us. We also need to remind ourselves that our future is something we constantly define and shape, not something that just happens to us.

To achieve this, we need to be curious and open, immerse ourselves in future scenarios, discover what it would be like to actually live in that future, connect to people that make the future happen, and increase our general awareness of the Zeitgeist that surrounds us. Assume less, discover more, and discard those toxic assumptions that worked so well in the past! Embrace the dramatic progress of science, but always see it in context of the overall human purpose. Technology can be heaven or hell, or both (#hellven), so we must be proactive and precautionary depending on how much is at stake, where and when.

2. **Our toughest challenges are often the most incredible opportunities (and vice versa).** Much of our future will hinge on that careful balance of magic and manic (but hopefully not toxic) use of technology. Because, as William Gibson suggests, technology is morally neutral until we apply it,[201] achieving balance will be more about orchestrating the applications and embodiments of technology than about preventing or even regulating the inventions themselves. The future is not about yes or no, it's about "it depends." I am certain that if we can allow the "why?" and "for what purpose?" questions to be voiced more often, a balanced approach will emerge.

3. **We must become much better stewards of humanity.** Every single business leader, technology pioneer, and public official needs to accept and act upon his/her responsibility for shaping the future of humanity. Civic and political leaders must develop a deep understanding and personal foresight about technology in the context of humanity, and become stewards of our collective future. Across all sectors of all industries, we will need a new kind of hyper-collaboration, not hyper-competition, and

we will need to think holistically across all those traditionally separate domains.

4. **Technology has no ethics, yet a society without ethics is doomed.** We are heading into a future where literally everything around us is impacted by a tsunami of technological advances, yet the way we frame the world, the way we evaluate what is right or wrong, the way we decide whether to engage and use a certain technology or not is still based on past experiences, on old frameworks, and worst of all, on linear thinking.

   Our ethics—and many of our laws and regulations as well—are still based on a world that advances linearly and on "what used to work" before we reached the pivot point on the exponential curve. Ever since the Internet became a significant commercial force, we seem to have focused in the main on exploiting its economic and commercial promises. We have spent way too little time considering its impact on our values and ethics—and this is finally becoming apparent as we enter the age of artificial intelligence (AI), robotics, and human genome editing.

   Recently, there has been growing discussion of the concept of building thinking machines that might be able to simulate human ethics. While this is an interesting twist, it strikes me as yet another step towards a wholly simulated machine age, and yet another reason why we need to establish a Global Digital Ethics Council. As we proceed towards the Singularity and the point at which computers reach or surpass the capability and capacity of the human brain, and are connected via a giant global network, we urgently need a clear ethical context that the majority of us can agree on. This is not an easy task, but one that is crucial to tackle, nevertheless.

5. **Beware: Exponential technologies often morph rapidly from magic to manic to toxic—achieving a balance is essential.** If you think that addiction to the Internet, to games,

to smartphones, or the pleasure traps of social networks is already a big issue, the full story has yet to unfold! Just wait until we can completely immerse ourselves in technology, until technology actually goes inside of us with augmented and virtual reality, brain-computer interfaces, implants, and neural interfaces.

The sky is literally the limit in terms of what exponential progress might make possible. Hence, we must now learn how to use technology holistically and with much greater respect for human ways and needs. We must also make those that invent, market, and provide these alluring new technological solutions responsible for the new ecosystems they empower, and look to them to offer effective ways to curb or limit unintended consequences. Technology providers must start including externalities in their business models, and need to help shape new social contracts that may address the toxic effects.

6. **We need to teach both STEM and CORE (compassion, originality, reciprocity, and empathy) skills.** Technology and humanity must both be on the curriculum; indeed science and philosophy belong in the same classroom. A balanced society will require expertise in both domains; otherwise, we will continue to tilt the playing field towards machine thinking.

   In addition, an increasing amount of scientific work will eventually be done by AI and smart machines; therefore, we must place the development of human-only skills and capabilities center-stage. Creativity, understanding, negotiation, questioning, emotions, intuition, and imagination will be more important than ever before—whatever cannot be digitized, automated, or virtualized will become extremely valuable.

7. **We need to retain a clear distinction between what is real and what is a copy or a simulation.** Total connectivity, thinking machines, the smart cloud, and cognitive computing are our inevitable future, yet we should not abandon the

distinction between simulation (machines) and being (*dasein*), between computation and sentience, between machine-kind and mankind. Immersing ourselves in a world of amazing simulations could be very useful for learning, entertainment, or work, but should it become the way we live, in general?

Could these technologies become a kind of universal drug that we will always crave to make our world more complete? Will we need limits and regulation on how much use we are allowed, and how deep we can go? If technology really isn't what we seek, but how we seek, we will need help to continue distinguishing between these tools and our true purpose? Building relationships with humans needs to remain more important than building relationships with machines. Embrace technology but don't become it.

8. **We need to start asking why and who, not just if or how.** Future strategic decisions about the development and deployment of technology should be more about sense-making, context, purpose, meaning, and relevance than simply focusing on feasibility, cost, scale, profits, and contributions to growth. The how question must be replaced by the why.

9. **We should not let Silicon Valley, technologists, the military, or investors become mission control for humanity—no matter what country they are in.** Those who fund, create, and sell exponential technologies are unlikely to be the ones who will want to curb their power or scale of potential applications. Those who build machines for war will not be those who will focus on human happiness. Those who invest in disruptive technologies to generate hundredfold returns will not be the ones who will invest in constructing the future of truly human societies for a collective benefit. Those that build the tools have their own agenda, and it's mostly about monetization and power—so where in the decision-making process is the representation of those that use the tools?

**Evaluating exponential technologies: seven essential questions to ask**

Given that much of this book is about how humanity could win in this impending battle with exponential technologies, here are seven questions I believe we must ask when evaluating the forces of radical change. I realize that in many cases the correct answer might be either "both" or "it depends." However, I feel that just by stopping to ask these questions, we might understand the trade-offs more clearly.

1. **Will this technology inadvertently or by design diminish humanity?** Will it seek to replace important human interactions that should not be intermediated by technology? Will it automate something uniquely human that really should not be automated? Does this technology liberate us from unnecessary and nonessential burdens, or does it tempt us to skip what is essentially human? Is it a wormhole or a catalyst?

2. **Will this technology further true human happiness?** Will it lead to making us more content with what we have, allow us to achieve more *eudaemonia*, and make a more connected contribution? Will it go far beyond simply providing hedonic pleasures, or if it is mostly a hedonistic tool, will it seek to lead us to confuse it with a deeper happiness?

3. **Does this technology have any unintended and potentially disastrous side effects?** Does it take authority away from us, collectively, or does it empower us? Will it have significant impact on ecosystems that are crucial to many people, and if so, does it include addressing those externalities in its business model?

4. **Will this technology give too much authority to itself or to other algorithms, bots, and machines?** Will users be tempted to abdicate their own authority by using it? Will we be encouraged to outsource our thinking to it? Will this technology serve us, or will it turn out to be mostly self-serving, i.e. mostly taking rather than giving value?

5. **Will this technology enable us to transcend it, i.e. go beyond itself, or will it make us dependent on it?** Will this technology force humans into a subordinate role, either by design or by accident? Will the technology so exceed our capabilities that we are forced into unquestioningly following its guidance and decisions?

6. **Will humans need to be materially changed or augmented to actually use this technology?** Is this technology leading us to upgrade our bodies or senses, or is it working within the existing confines of who we are? Will it force us to upgrade and augment if we want access to jobs, education, and healthcare?

7. **Will this technology be openly available, or will it be proprietary?** Can we tinker with it, or will it be locked? Will it be available to everyone, or only the top 1%? Will it increase inequality, or serve to lessen it? How will we know the scale of wealth being amassed by the dominant providers if technology controls our access to the information?

## Are you on Team Human?

I first heard this powerful meme from Douglas Rushkoff,[202] and immediately thought it would make an excellent motto on our journey towards the future.

This is what "Being on Team Human" means to me:

- To put our collective human flourishing first and above all other concerns;
- To allow androrithms, those uniquely human things such as imagination, chance, mistakes, and inefficiencies, to continue to matter, even if they are undesired by or incompatible with technology;
- To fight the spread of machine thinking, i.e. not to change what we stand for and need as humans because it might make it easier for the technologies that surround us;

- Not to be tempted into preferring technological magic, i.e. great simulations of reality over reality itself, and not to get addicted to technology;
- Not to prefer relationships with screens and machines over those that we can have with fellow humans.

As I said at the start, my aim has been to highlight the challenges, start the debate, and provoke a spirited response. What will you do to further the conversation in your organization, community, family, and friendship circles?

For my part, I will continue to investigate what being on Team Human means through my ongoing work as a keynote speaker, advisor, writer, and filmmaker. Please join the discussion on the book's website www.techvshuman.com, and on the www.onteamhuman. com microsite.

# Acknowledgements

This book would not have come to fruition had it not been for the support of all these great people.

My dear wife, **Angelica Feldmann**, who lovingly endured my physical and/or mental absence during the last 18 months, provided much needed honest critique, and supported me all the way.

**Jean Francois Cardella**, producer and art director and overall creative advisor and friend.

**Francois Mazoudier** for his honest feedback and his friendship

**James McCabe** for his amazing scriptwriting and further editing

**Rohit Talwar, Steve Wells and April Koury**—the team at Fast Future Publishing—for their enthusiasm, rigorous and forensic editorial focus, and willingness to act at exponential speed to turn the raw manuscript into a finished product.

**David Battino** for developmental editing

**Maggie Langrick** for her initial structural edits and overall advice

The crew at **Like.Digital** in London, for building the www.techvshuman.com site.

**Benjamin Blust**, my webmaster and technical director

## On the Shoulders of Giants

This book is inspired by the work of many visionaries—authors and writers, speakers, thinkers, personalities, business leaders, and filmmakers. Thanks to all of you!

Here is just the tip of that iceberg:

| | |
|---|---|
| James Barrat | Andrew Keen |
| Yochai Benkler | Kevin Kelly |
| Nick Bostrom | Ray Kurzweil |
| Richard Branson | Jaron Lanier |
| David Brin | Larry Lessig |
| Erik Brynjoffson | John Markoff |
| Nicholas Carr | Andrew McAfee |
| Noam Chomsky | Elon Musk |
| Paulo Coelho | Thomas Piketty |
| The Dalai Lama | Jeremy Rifkin |
| Peter Diamandis | Charlie Rose |
| Philip K. Dick | Douglas Rushkoff |
| Cory Doctorow | Clay Shirky |
| Dave Eggers | Tiffany Shlain |
| John Elkington | Edward Snowden |
| William Gibson | Don Tapscott |
| Daniel Kahneman | |

# Resources

References, including hyperlinks to source content can be found on the dedicated page for *Technology vs. Humanity* on the Fast Future Publishing website at
www.fastfuturepublishing.com/main/books/tech-vs-human

You can join the social media discussion on *Technology vs. Humanity* and find further content here:

| | |
|---|---|
| Facebook | www.facebook.com/techvshuman |
| LinkedIn | www.linkedin.com/groups/12002283 |
| Twitter | www.twitter.com/techvshuman |
| Gerd's regular updates | www.techvshuman.com |
| Team Human | www.onteamhuman.com |

Further information on Gerd Leonhard and his work:

| | |
|---|---|
| Gerd's show reel: | www.gerd.io/2016ShowReel |
| The Futures Agency: | www.thefuturesagency.com |
| English Website: | www.futuristgerd.com |
| German Website: | www.gerdleonhard.de |
| Newsletter sign-up: | www.gerd.io/getgerdsnews |
| Twitter: | www.twitter.com/gleonhard |
| Facebook: | www.facebook.com/gleonhard |
| LinkedIn | https://ch.linkedin.com/in/gleonhard |
| | |
| Contact: | gerd@thefuturesagency.com |

# Fast Future Publishing

We are a new breed of publisher founded by three futurists - Rohit Talwar, Steve Wells, and April Koury. Our goal is to profile the latest thinking of established and emerging futurists, foresight researchers, and future thinkers from around the world, and to make those ideas accessible to the widest possible audience in the shortest possible time.

Our FutureScapes book series is designed to address a range of critical agenda setting futures topics that we believe are relevant to individuals, governments, businesses, and civil society. *Technology vs. Humanity* is the second book in the series.

Our first book, *The Future of Business*, provides 60 fast moving chapters and 566 pages of cutting-edge thinking from 62 future thinkers in 21 different countries on four continents. Traditional publishers would take two years to deliver a book of this magnitude; we completed the journey from idea to publication in just 19 weeks.

We have also created an innovative business model that bypasses most of the traditional publishing practices and inefficiencies, embracing digital era exponential thinking and applying it to transform the publishing process, the distribution approach, and the profit sharing model.

Our publishing model ensures that our authors, core team members, and partners on each book share in its profits. Additionally, a proportion of profits are allocated to a development fund to finance causes related to the core topic. For *The Future of Business*, the fund will be used to finance scholarships for those wanting to take courses in foresight research and practice. For *Technology vs. Humanity* the fund will be targeted at initiatives that seek to further the debate.

We hope that our story and our approach to publishing are an inspiring example of how business is evolving and being reinvented in the digital era.

Over the coming years, Fast Future Publishing aims to publish the work of insightful and inspiring futurists and future thinkers. We are keen to receive proposals from potential authors and those interested in compiling and editing multi-contributor book as part of the FutureScapes series.

For corporate or bulk orders of *Technology vs. Humanity* or *The Future of Business*, to explore partnership opportunities, to submit a book proposal, to discuss curating a multi-contributor project, or to enquire about permanent and internship opportunities, we can be reached at info@fastfuturepublishing.com.

You can learn more about us at www.fastfuturepulishing.com.

We look forward to hearing from you!